compassion
is the key to
everything

Sarah O' Brien

About the Author

Alexandra Chauran is a second-generation fortune teller. As a professional psychic intuitive for over a decade, she serves thousands of clients in the Seattle area and globally through her website. She is certified in tarot and has been interviewed on National Public Radio and other major media outlets. Alexandra is currently pursuing a doctoral degree, lives in Issaquah, Washington, and can be found online at SeePsychic.com.

compassion
is the key to
everything

Find Your Own Path

ALEXANDRA CHAURAN

Llewellyn Publications
Woodbury, Minnesota

FIRST EDITION
First Printing, 2016

Book design by Bob Gaul
Cover art by iStockphoto.com/4645860/©Zeno0620
Cover design by Ellen Lawson
Editing by Laura Graves

Llewellyn Publications is a registered trademark of Llewellyn Worldwide Ltd.

Library of Congress Cataloging-in-Publication Data
Chauran, Alexandra, 1981–
Compassion is the key to everything: find your own path/Alexandra Chauran. First Edition.
    pages cm
Includes bibliographical references.
ISBN 978-0-7387-4667-8
1. Compassion. 2. Parapsychology. 3. Occultism. I. Title.
BJ1475.C43 2016
177'.7—dc23
                            2015034863

Llewellyn Publications
A Division of Llewellyn Worldwide Ltd.
2143 Wooddale Drive
Woodbury, MN 55125-2989
www.llewellyn.com

Printed in the United States of America

This book is dedicated to Janet Delpierre, who chose to be a living kidney donor. In doing so, Janet gave my mother the gift of life, gave me my healthy mother back, and gave my children the ability to meet and know their Grandma Jean. The ripples of compassion Janet spread through the universe for just one kind woman's life will never end.

Table of Contents

Five:

Becoming a Beacon
of Kindness for Others . . . 179

'Tis a gift to be simple, 'tis a gift to be free
'Tis a gift to come down where we ought to be,
And when we find ourselves in the place just right,
'Twill be in the valley of love and delight.
When true simplicity is gain'd,
To bow and to bend we shan't be asham'd,
To turn, turn will be our delight,
Till by turning, turning we come 'round right.

—*Quaker Hymn "Simple Gifts"*—

Introduction

You already know that when all is said and done and you're finally finished with this lifetime on earth, your last thoughts won't be about your accumulated possessions. You know that you won't be showing off any college degrees on the wall or even telling stories about incredible travels. Instead, your thoughts and plans will center on those last moments with your loved ones. Relationships are what matter in life, and empathy and compassion are at the root of all loving relationships.

It was a conversation about compassion with my father that influenced my view of how important it is to nurture this attitude of giving to others. We were talking about my husband, then fiancé, and I was trying to explain to Dad why I had chosen to marry this man over all others. As I was wringing my hands in the presence of an overprotective father, my brain was going a mile a minute trying to calculate all the things Dad might admire, respect, or value about this young man. My dad interrupted me with a single, gentle question: "Is he kind to you?" At the heart of it, my dad intuitively knew that his most precious daughter should be with someone who possessed this virtue above all others. Presented here is a guide to discovering this jewel of peace within yourself and sharing it with others.

Why Compassion?

Nearly all the world's faiths and spiritual traditions have some imperative to "harm none" or minimize harm in some way, whether it be to others or to oneself. My own guidance comes from a rede, or advice, by Gwen Thompson that says: "An' it harm none, do what ye will." Now, many interpret this phrase as a proactive one rather than restrictive. This means that if you want to do something and it doesn't harm anybody, go ahead and do it. But this interpretation can release someone from some of the "harm none" component, as it says nothing about the situations in which harm happens when a person isn't actively doing what he or she wants to do—only the certain circumstances in which a person truly wants to do something that harms none. This interpretation may sound like an ethical stretch, but many philosophies and sacred texts seem to allow for loopholes. So why do people work so hard to interpret the teachings of the world's religions as allowing harm? Because harming none is next to impossible, and yet we still want to encourage people to strive toward that ideal.

The directive to avoid harm includes the self, reducing dangers and injuries inflicted upon one's own life. So far so good; avoiding self-harm sounds like a no-brainer. Not harming other people can also have some wonderful benefits. Peace between people increases our personal safety as well as our ability to collaborate and find joy together. Best of all, harming none makes the individual practitioner more mindful of his or her actions. Instead of moving robotically through life, we weigh the consequences of actions carefully and assume a place of power through personal responsibility.

The Golden Rule

The Golden Rule comes in many forms in many different faiths. The gist of the Golden Rule is that you should only act toward others in a way that you would like others to act toward you. The scriptures of the world religions each phrase this in different ways but with the same thought at its heart. Treating others kindly helps others treat you nicely, and this action sends a ripple of kindness throughout the world. The Golden Rule is a discipline available for all spiritual people to embrace. When I get through a day minimizing harm to others and spreading kindness as a natural reaction, I find myself experiencing a special sort of spiritual joy. This spiritual state is what mythologist Joseph Campbell called following your bliss. The way ahead in life, though complicated and messy, is met with a light heart and a spirit of hope. As you read ahead, consider strongly the responsibility to harm none and also follow your bliss.

Gwen Thompson, as mentioned before, encouraged many to do what they truly desired to do as long as no one would be harmed. She and other spiritual thinkers painted the picture of "harm none" as a law that was difficult to follow but rewarding: adherents could find freedom to follow their bliss without the curse of negative consequences. What sort of negative consequences? The outcome varies across religions significantly, even though the goal of harming none is the same. Some believe there will be divine or universal retribution carried out as a matter of course. Just as every action has an equal and opposite reaction, it is thought that harm can be visited back upon the perpetrator, sometimes to an unequal or extreme degree.

The Golden Rule can also be seen as a directive about empathy. You are probably reading this because you're a naturally empathetic person. If you see somebody suffering, you naturally want to relieve that suffering in some way, even if it means taking on some suffering yourself. Empathy can be a blessing and a curse, however. The empathetic person is uniquely suited to reduce harm in the world. He or she sees harm being caused and can become a problem-solver as well as a comforting influence.

Empathy can turn on itself and become a problem, however. Overly empathetic people may seem like real downers to friends and family. As empathetic people are so attuned to suffering, friends and family may have to hear about that negativity more often and may feel sad or frustrated because of it. Empathetic people may also choose to take on suffering when it is unnecessary and does not solve the problem. These are all clues that the empathic person has skipped the vital problem-solving part of the equation and instead is becoming overwhelmed by the suffering he or she feels.

If you find yourself being weighed down by your own empathy, it can feel like the world is against you. You are working so hard at doing to others what you would want done to you, and in response you may be avoided, yelled at, or surrounded by pouty and negative people who resist your efforts at every turn. There are a couple things you can do: If you are an empathetic person and nobody will listen, it's time to get a therapist. Working with a mental health professional can train you to switch gears to problem-solving mode or avoid stimuli that set off your empathy alarms. If you're not being triggered by all the suffering in the world, you will have more mental space and time to take action in smaller and more practical ways to reduce suffering.

After addressing your mental health needs, consider turning to spirit. For millennia, humanity has turned to the divine when nothing else can be done. If you're overwhelmed, it means that nothing can be done at this time. When nothing practical can be done, pray or meditate. Open your heart to the divine and lay out the pain you have taken on. You can ask for comfort and relief, or you can just express the inexpressible. Your relationship with divinity can strengthen your boundaries and perhaps help you realize the purpose for your empathy.

What Lies Ahead

You'll need to know what is at the heart of living with compassion before you come up with your own game plan. So, we'll begin with an exploration of your own empathy and compassion. After this basic groundwork, you'll be encouraged to question your own motives behind this selfless quest of giving to others. Your actions should originate from your life's purpose at all times. Then, you can begin the methodical process of changing your life, whether that means getting your life back on track or making some gentle adjustments to nurture a peaceful existence. I'll also give you some ideas for spreading your passion for compassion to others without sounding too preachy.

My Case in Point

It was New Year's Eve when I nervously conveyed to my husband my resolution to live a year of "harm none." He knew, you see, that I had a somewhat ambivalent attitude regarding ethics and morals. I'd been known to bristle when people claimed to be living a more ethical or moral life than the rest of society. As a middle-aged wife and mother, I came to realize that we're all just trying to do our best in a busy and sometimes nonsensical world. Still, I had a hunger inside of me to become a more ethical person. I figured that a yearning like this shouldn't be ignored. My list of New Year's resolutions has always looked like a laundry list of a terribly guilty person, as I've tried desperately to shake the dust from my life.

Supportive though he is, my husband rolled his eyes and groaned when my resolutions came into play. He told me that he didn't believe in New Year's resolutions, offering the alternative that one should make self-improvement efforts all year long and that changes should be implemented the moment they come to mind. That sounded reasonable enough to me, although I liked the extra motivation of the cultural tradition of resolutions. My husband was also annoyed by my annual ethical crisis because some of my resolutions would inevitably affect him negatively. In truth, nearly everything we do affects others; our actions have a ripple effect on the universe. Despite his protests, it was time to empower myself with knowledge and action to change my little corner of the world.

Fast forward through a year of making mistakes, learning some lessons, and continuous research. I've found myself feeling better about my place in the world, and people around me are thanking me for becoming a little less self-centered. The resulting bonus from that struggle is the book you now hold in your hands. I may not be Mother Teresa, but I've set a personal record for compassion while working on it. If others like me are working toward this same goal—and I know many of you are—we can all make the world a better place together.

The real work of compassion is to go beyond ideology. Sure, systemic problems can and should be addressed, but there are so many more practical issues of harm that can happen in the average person's everyday experience. Harm happens in our relationships, when the wrong words slip out when speaking to a stranger, and when we ignore our very real obligations in life in favor of distractions or ideologies. I harm my husband when I ignore him when he's trying to share something important with me. I harm my children if I yell at them instead of digging deep into my patience and teaching them the lessons they need to learn. Life isn't as simple as buying the most ethically responsible brand of milk or car. The real work in "harm none," therefore, is simultaneously easy and difficult: we aren't necessarily required to make a complete overhaul of what we do with our possessions, but it is always difficult to transform the way we view the world and interact with it.

one

Getting Along With Others Without Beating Yourself Up

My four-year-old daughter had a really rough day at preschool today. She got into another fight with one of her friends and even ended up taking a scratch to the face. In the car ride home she was snarky and miserable, trying every excuse to pick a fight with me. I stayed quiet, praying the car wouldn't erupt into a screaming match between my two kids with kicks flying between the car seats. When we arrived home, I ran off to get started on dinner and left the children to their own devices. Perhaps that was my mistake—I should have taken a moment to reconnect with her. Soon enough, however, she let me know that she needed attention.

I heard her shouting at her little two-year-old brother in the other room. Her voice was strained. I turned off the stove top and went into the room to see what was going on. My toddler son was being himself, playing with a toy airplane while sitting in a little red wagon. My daughter's face was streaked with tears as she told me about how he just wasn't doing everything that she told him to do. She was trying to direct his play, and he wasn't cooperating with her micromanagement. I could see her issue for what it really was: she was feeling out of control in her life and so now was trying to exert control anywhere and everywhere else.

I gave her a hug and told her a story about a man who went to work and had a bad day because his boss said something mean to him. When the man got home, he was so mad that he kicked his dog. At this point in the story, my daughter gave an appropriate gasp of alarm. She rightfully knew that the man was doing something wrong by kicking the dog. I tucked one of her braids behind her ear and explained gently that when she comes home from school after having a bad day and is mean to her little brother, it's like the man in the story. We then talked about what she might want to do to get some space away from her brother while she decompressed.

The value of compassionate living manifests in relationships with the greatest impact. I can agonize over whether my life choices harm generations in the future, people in far off lands, or animals, but the real harm I usually cause is in every-day conversations with my children and husband especially, as well as conversations with acquaintances and strangers. We all know that words can cause harm. They're so powerful, they can convict a person of a crime or deliver scarring, lasting emotional wounds. Negative words can attract negativity into our lives. The result is a snowball effect, where the negative things you think and say cause you to notice more negativity around you and possibly even draw more bad people and awful events into your life. In this way, harming people with words visits that harm upon our own lives.

Relational harm is usually a deeply ingrained habit, often with roots in childhood. Many children learn their interactive word patterns early by observing the grown-ups. It's not their fault that they grow up emulating verbally abusive patterns, but even people from abusive childhoods can change their ways. If any abuse is in your past and you struggle with it, never fear—you can break free from the cycle. For those of you with severe issues, you may want the help of a therapist. An expert can walk you through what triggers your urge to lash out verbally and what alternative actions you can take.

For the rest of us, nasty words can be blurted out by even the nicest person. Triggers can be tiredness, hunger, stress, and many other things. Figuring out your triggers may be the first step. Solving those problems before you interact with people can be the simplest solution. It may require walking away from a frustrating conversation, excusing yourself and saying, "I need a breather. Can we talk about this later?" Then you can come back to it when you're feeling better able to control what you say.

Swearing Off Snark and Vain or Foolish Conversation

They say that reading or watching news makes people fearful. If you see images of people being hurt all the time, your brain will naturally start telling you that the world is a dangerous place. I find this same phenomenon happens to me when I take in media showing verbal or relational harm. We all know that it's probably not a good idea for little kids to watch television programs with rude words and phrases, and as it turns out, I've noticed a change in my behavior when I take in that sort of media too. Maybe the same happens for you.

I used to have a guilty pleasure of reading comedy blogs online that make fun of people. Participating in these snarky and catty communities where people comment with cruel jokes used to be a diversion in my day. Over time, however, I noticed that reading those blogs made me snarkier and more sarcastic in real life. I made jokes at my husband's expense to friends, and I made assumptions that others around me weren't as smart as they seemed. When I ran into problems with words in my relationships, I decided to swear off those blogs and other media sources of snark and rudeness. Taking a break for a week turned into a month, and I'm now going on several months. Doing so really made a difference in how I react in conversations. Instead of making my husband the butt of my jokes, I now remind myself that I want to uplift him in all conversations and help him be the best person he can be. This, in turn, helps me become a better person.

Consider sources of media that might be causing you to automatically assume people around you are stupid, or that mean, snarky comments are good entertainment. Are there television shows or websites that may be influencing you? Can you take a break from those media and see if it influences the way you talk to others? Experiment and see if you notice a difference.

Of course, media isn't the only source of these kinds of influences. Many of us are influenced even more by the conversations all around us between family, coworkers, and friends. It's not practical to be the thought police and stop all the negative conversations from happening, but you can opt out of participating in them. For this task, I like to take a page from *The Key of Solomon* by S. Liddell MacGregor Mathers. In his instructions for magical practitioners, he suggests that one abstain from "vain and foolish conversation" for a period of time. He suggests nine days, but to be honest, I don't think I could manage to abstain that long. Instead, I try to abstain from those sorts of conversation for three days before each sacred holiday in my life.

So, what constitutes "vain and foolish conversation"? All religious traditions agree that gossip is bad, so it is the first thing to go when I take a break from negative conversations. If I want to talk about somebody else who is not in my company, I talk to that person directly instead. If I hear other people around me gossiping, I stay silent. If it is my place to do so, I ask the people not to gossip and to wait to discuss the topic until the person in question is present.

Vanity refers to prideful boasting that serves no good purpose. Vanity can bring our attention away from the needs of others. Remaining attentive to the needs of others is an important part of compassionate living. Vanity can also make others feel emotionally hurt in many contexts, such as when we brag in a way that makes others feel sad about their own lack in life. You might not have the problems with vanity that I do, but try to check bragging if and when it does occur.

Foolish or silly conversations have their time and place. Giggling with friends over nonsense can be a perfectly harmless activity. However, if your conversations mostly revolve around nonsense and foolishness, it can bring attention away from the more serious and spiritual questions of life. I notice that when I avoid foolish conversations, I tend to ask the people in my life important questions. I talk about deeper world troubles and life goals or ask people, "How are you?" and really mean it. It's nice to take a break from sillier conversations for a few days preceding a holiday or other spiritual event. If you don't celebrate any sacred holidays, you can pick any old time. I tend to try to abstain from foolish conversations about twice a month. It's pretty funny when my husband and I are talking and I get to say, "I can't help but notice that this conversation is incredibly foolish and I must abstain!" The silly talk we're having always gets one last laugh from us both. You may or may not find this practice useful for you. I find it resets my attitude every once in a while, especially if I've fallen into a pattern of only thinking about myself and my own amusement when talking to others.

Speaking and Listening

Balancing speaking and listening can reduce harm in all your relationships. We've all been in those arguments where instead of truly listening to the other person, we are much more focused on what to say in order to win the argument. Not listening can cause damage over time if neither person listens to the other. Taking turns speaking and listening is a skill they're teaching my child in preschool, and it is one that adults like myself still struggle with on a daily basis.

In Gwen Thompson's poem about living a virtuous life, she wrote: "Soft of eye and light of touch; speak little, listen much." Many people have a natural inclination to talk much more than listen. The pairing of the words in this couplet paint a picture of a person who acts with true compassion: the eyes are "soft"; that is, looking into another person's eyes with kindness. One of the most important skills a good listener has is the ability to make appropriate eye contact. A "light touch" is a metaphor for gentle words, calling to mind the image of laying a friendly and comforting hand on somebody as they speak. Bring this imagery to mind whenever somebody is angry or upset when speaking to you. Try to take the form of the good listener. Wait and allow the person to vent emotions, even if what the person says does not align with the facts as you know them. After venting, the person may be more ready to apologize or listen to reason than if you had interrupted, fired back immediately, or "corrected" their recollection of events.

Good listening can also mean paraphrasing or asking important questions when appropriate. If a person is telling you a story, you might find yourself internally trying to relate the story to another story that *you* can tell. Instead, ask questions that show interest and curiosity. Find something interesting about what the person is saying and ask further questions about it. You'll help the person feel good about themself and good about you.

If you sometimes struggle with conversation topics for friends and strangers alike, there's a mnemonic to help remember some topics so you can ask simple questions and get right back to listening. Just remember FORD: Family, Occupation, Recreation, and Dreams. I find this little trick especially helpful when trying to abstain from more frivolous conversation. If the person is a stranger, I can ask him or her about family. If the person is a friend, I can ask a more targeted question, such as "How's your husband's job hunt going?" People like to talk about their jobs, so asking questions about how their occupations work can be very interesting and fulfilling. Asking about recreation can get people talking about things that make them happy. "Are you traveling anywhere for the holidays?" It's fun to watch their eyes light up as they relate their plans. My favorite thing to talk about is their dreams for the future. "What do you hope to do after you retire?" Or I ask, "Where would you like to travel that you haven't yet visited?" Learning the answers to some of these questions, even from strangers, can keep me engaged in the conversation so much that trying to be a good listener no longer feels like a chore.

Overall, being a good listener is all about balance. You don't have to take a vow of silence to let others talk. Silence does have its place and will be addressed later in this chapter, but don't simply practice being mute for now. Practice drawing out other peoples' ideas through active listening and questioning. You'll learn more about what others around you like and don't like, and that can help you be more sensitive to their needs so you can avoid accidentally harming them through hurtful words or actions. You might find out that your friend hates chocolate or that your brother always wanted to take a trip to Las Vegas. Listening well is a habit that takes time to develop and see the benefits of. The result is worth it: soon you'll get a reputation as caring without having done more than nod your head at the right moments. Over time, you'll notice that you grow a bigger heart for those around you once you listen to their greatest hopes and dreams.

Active Listening Exercise

Active listening means engaging in the experience of listening to what somebody else has to say without thinking about what you're planning to say next. It can be a challenge, as humans are hard-wired to categorize everything and make connections between our lives and observations in order to keep the world interesting. The problem happens when this constant egocentric processing takes away from the power of the person sharing his or her story, concerns, or other important words.

There are several easy ways to be an active listener. The first is to go into the conversation with the right attitude. It's difficult to head into an argument with a loved one planning to be an active listener because you're going to be too invested in getting your point of view across. Today, choose a time when you will be an active listener. A good time to practice is when there are no major problems between you and the other person. For example, consider talking to your partner when he or she comes home from work, a child when he or she comes home from school, or calling a parent on the phone to catch up. Pick a person with whom you generally don't have constant power struggles.

Before you start your active listening conversation, think about what active listening looks like, feels like, and sounds like. Ideally, you'll practice active listening in person. You can use body language to show that you are listening to the other person by making eye contact, showing appropriate facial expressions to match the other person's emotions, and nodding along when you agree with what the other person is saying. Keeping your body facing the other person's body and your arms and legs uncrossed sends the message that you're open to what the other person is saying and also may allow the two of you to exchange energy more freely.

Remember: active listening isn't entirely silent. Yes, you're going to give the other person plenty of time to speak without interruption. However, you can also engage in the conversation by asking clarifying questions or restating the other person's ideas in your own words. Resist the urge to take the conversation on a tangent topic that is more related to your own life or experiences. Ask questions like, "What happened next?" or "What did you think about that?" If anything sounds unclear when you're listening, try explaining your own understanding of what has been said by saying something like, "It sounds like you're saying that…" or "In other words, you mean…" and let the other person clarify if needed.

Now that you have an idea of what your active listening will be like, dive in and give it a try. Remember to enter the conversation without any plans to talk about your own topics. Give yourself over to the moment. When the conversation is finished, reflect on how you did. You may find that your mind wandered or you were tempted to shift the topic of conversation. It's okay if you did; active listening takes practice. If you're an assertive person you may have years of habits to break. However, you may have also noticed some of the benefits of active listening such as connecting with the other person's joy or other emotions, and helping the other person feel important. Give yourself regular opportunities to practice active listening.

True Love and a Warm Heart

One trait of being compassionate, an idea put forth by religions all over the world, is the idea of loving everyone. This is obviously problematic. Not only are there plenty of people in the world that you might actively dislike, but the vast majority of people in the world are strangers. It is difficult for anyone to automatically love a stranger. We've evolved to care for our close family and to view potential rivals with suspicion. To understand the virtue of loving strangers, it's time to back up and understand the nature of love in the context of the religious cultures from which these ideas and philosophies were drawn.

In my religion and in the sacred scriptures of others, "perfect love" is the ideal. This may seem strange to anyone who has experienced the messy, chaotic, often dramatic everyday love of marriage, friendship, and family. My husband and I love each other very much, but both of us are far from perfect. Even the pure love I felt for my kids when I first laid eyes on them is colored in my memory by the petty squabbles of family life. This doesn't mean that the love is not "perfect" in the divine sense of the word. Perhaps perfect love is imperfect by its very design, forcing us to examine our actions and words at every turn.

"Perfect" is a loaded term for us perfectionists, so let's call the ideal love for everyone "true love" for a moment. Love for everyone should be honest and authentic, but it certainly doesn't have to match the intensity or any other characteristic of love for one's child, parent, or spouse. In other words, you don't have to feel guilty about the quality or quantity of love you have for strangers—there's no purpose for that particular guilt. True love must be carefully nurtured, as it can be damaged easily by something like a breach of trust.

Consider the benefits of loving others in the world. If you give love to many people in the world, you multiply the positive energy of love in your life. This is one manifestation of the law of attraction, or how like energies attract like. A loving attitude can draw more love into your life and cause others to love you. This is good news for people searching for that special someone.

Another benefit to loving others around you is that the world becomes a generally happier place. Suddenly, even when you're surrounded by strangers, it is as if you're surrounded by friends. You can feel joy when you see happy strangers. You can feel like help is only an arm's reach away if you ever need assistance. The fear generated by watching violence on the news can dim, dull, and even disappear from your life.

Like the concept of "harming none," the goal of loving everyone flirts with impossibility. Don't try to love every criminal you see in the newspaper just yet; go easy on yourself. Start with your neighbors, acquaintances, colleagues, and all the other faces that move in and out of your life. You fake it until you make it. Start by smiling. Smiling can actually make you feel happy, if you practice it enough. It's a tough practice, but a good one. Once you form the habit of smiling at strangers, it becomes easier.

Try this trick the next time you're talking to an exasperating coworker or family member. Think to yourself, "I like you." Think it quietly, over and over again, as you watch him or her speak. It may seem silly and disingenuous, but you may find it works magic. Your shoulders may relax, and so may your expectations. Perhaps you're less likely to snap at the person and more likely to listen to what he or she has to say. The interaction may even become one between friends instead of adversaries. If you know the person, try thinking about one thing you like about him or her. It can be the person's honesty, sense of humor, or even his or her personal style. The point of the exercise is to stop fixating on things you might dislike about an interaction and to start focusing on the positive.

It turns out that meditation can be a powerful tool to help you think positively about people and about your life. In a study on meditating about compassion, one group of subjects meditated on compassion for just twenty-five minutes. Those who meditated about compassion were able to recall significantly more positive words in a verbal learning test than a different group that just listened to relaxing music instead (Wheeler and Lenick, 11). If you focus on compassion, you think more positively about the world and remember more good things about your own life. This effect can snowball into a happier and more compassionate life. Another study that looked at whether compassion was something that could be learned or trained discovered that the amount of meditation practiced was associated with increased self-compassion and compassion for others (Jazaieri et al., 1113). Meditation is an important part of developing a compassionate lifestyle.

Here's a spiritual meditation you can use, though I strongly urge you to try the practical application of loving others before you start any spiritual practices. Spiritual practices support your psychosocial practices and vice versa. Eventually they join. If you're an introvert like me, you'd rather sit in a garden alone meditating all day rather than getting down to the business of human social interaction. But of course, our goal here is making tough decisions until they're part of the daily routine.

The following meditation can be done solo or in a group. After having my first child, I remember how lonely I felt at night when I was taking my turn to soothe the baby, pacing the hallways in the darkness. But then I thought about all the other mothers, fathers, grandparents, and others who were comforting a fussing newborn baby at that moment in time. It must have been quite a few. I didn't feel lonely anymore. While you practice this meditation, imagine all the other people who are praying and meditating for world peace and brotherly love at the same moment in time as you.

Wrapping the World in Love Meditation

Seat yourself comfortably and focus on your breathing. Know that the air you breathe is the air you share with everyone else on the planet. Keep breathing normally, and now imagine you're breathing in positive energy and breathing out any harmful energy. You can visualize this energy exchange happening in your chest, right around where your heart is located. What does this energy look like to you? Does it look like light, beads, smoke, or something else? What color is it?

Imagine what it would look like if you were floating above your body looking down on yourself. If you see the energy as a glowing light, imagine that light as you zoom out to look at your neighborhood, your city, your country, your world.

Imagine all the other points of lights on the planet as other people who are also meditating or praying for love in the world right at this moment.

Visualize your love spreading over the world. What does it look like to you? Does it look like you're wrapping the planet in a hand-knitted shawl? Does it look like a ribbon of light? Allow yourself a few moments to feel the love streaming out from your heart to the world. Relax your muscles and let it flow. You may feel a peaceful feeling come over you. When you are finished, open your eyes and see if you can still feel the connection with other loving people in the world. Thank them quietly and then go about your day as usual.

Compassion

We now delve into the virtues found in religious traditions all over the world, and the first that comes to mind is compassion. Compassion is an important spiritual virtue that allows us to see the suffering we are meant to prevent, and it is more than mere empathy, although empathy can be an important tool for compassion. Empathy is the ability to feel what others are feeling. Sympathy is the ability to have a heart for those who are suffering. It is possible to have sympathy for someone without having to share their pain, as one who has empathy might.

Speaking of suffering, here's another ethical and spiritual question: Is it better to suffer with the suffering? Or is it enough to simply try to relieve the suffering of others? Different religions answer this question in different ways through parables, some of which glorify the idea of sacrifice and suffering for others, and others that encourage reaching out with helping hands even if no harm befalls the compassionate person. Perhaps both empathy and compassion can be spiritually beneficial but in different ways. It might not seem like it, but empathy can be a double-edged sword: the ability to relate so closely to others and to suffer when they suffer can negatively affect one's personal ability to mitigate that suffering. You need to be generous to yourself and not cause yourself harm while creating your own compassionate lifestyle.

Self-compassion can actually increase the ability to be mindful of others, but being nice to yourself does take practice. In one study on self-compassion, subjects who practiced self-compassion for only three weeks were 21 percent successful in making significant gains in self-compassion, and they increased their mindfulness to boot (Smeets et al. 800–802). Imagine what would happen if you were to make self-compassion a lifelong practice—the good news is that you can become an expert starting today.

Compassion without any degree of empathy can still include sympathy. Consider the sympathetic doctor who helps patients deal with cancer without having to weep bitterly for each one who doesn't make it through treatment. Such people are often called to healing paths because they are able to deal with the flood of emotions that comes with witnessing pain. It may not feel right to dismiss suffering people outright when one is unable to deal with that sadness, but this is the only way some people are able to protect themselves emotionally. While controlling sadness and the outpouring of sympathy are necessary for vulnerable people, it can block opportunities for compassion. At the other end of the spectrum, a complete lack of empathy may make it impossible to feel compassion even when given the opportunity. If you can't feel another's pain, it is hard to imagine their suffering or even recognize it.

In *Men are From Mars, Women are From Venus*, author John Gray famously wrote that women seek sympathy and empathy when they have problems whereas men simply wish to solve the problem. Of course, this is a false dichotomy: not only do women and men fail to fit neatly into these categories, but it discounts the reality that every individual probably falls somewhere along an ever-changing, context-sensitive spectrum. Compassion can be easy to come by even for the most cold and stoic of "Martians," and even diehard "Venusians" can feel a desire to get to the bottom of a problem. The fact that Dr. Gray is even trying to solve the issue of communication differences between the sexes is evidence of some form of sympathy that can be understood as compassion.

Regardless of where you fall along the spectrum of responses to the suffering of others, you might benefit from having both a problem-solving and sympathetic approach. If you feel compassion for another, you don't need to wallow empathetically with the person, but you can tell him or her that you feel sadness about the situation and offer a possible solution if one is available. If no solution is available, sympathy may be all you have to offer along with prayer or heartfelt love.

Compassion Exercise

The exercise for this virtue isn't a specific meditation but rather an exercise of perspective. You can try a few angles. When meeting somebody who is expressing suffering, you may already try to picture yourself in his or her situation. Try to imagine this completely with somebody in your life who may be suffering in a way that you can't understand. Imagine having that person's resources, that person's history, and that person's coping skills. This can help you have compassion for people who may not be handling things as maturely or smoothly as you believe you would. For example, a young man just entering college may not be able to handle a breakup and dividing belongings between himself and his live-in girlfriend as well as somebody in midlife who had experienced more breakups. He might suffer more deeply and feel less capable of handling the task. Instead of dismissing his suffering as silly or pointless, it may help to understand that this may be the worst loss he has ever experienced, and that he may have no family nearby or other resources to provide ways to cope.

Another way to have compassion for strangers is to imagine someone is your close friend or even your child. This can help when you might otherwise assume the worst of a suffering person. For example, if somebody stole your lunch out of the office fridge, you might immediately feel rage and a lack of sympathy. You might even consider them a criminal, if you are hungry enough! But if you imagine that person is your best friend or child, you might have more sympathy. You might be more willing to allow that person a mistake and to talk to him or her with kindness and compassion. These simple exercises aren't cure-alls for instant compassion, but they are the beginnings of the basics if you've struggled with finding compassion in the past. If you find yourself unable to feel sufficient compassion for a specific group of people, volunteering with or for that population might help you connect with them and relate to them more.

Kindness

Kindness is considered a virtue across so many religious faiths, and many stories portray the expression of kindness in ways that require selflessness. However, kindness doesn't always have to be selfless. Sometimes it can serve the person being kind as much as the person receiving the act of kindness. Best of all, kindness is essentially a harm-reducing act: it eliminates the emotional harm of unkindness and can even cheer somebody up who is suffering for some other reason. My spiritual tradition and many others believe that kindness is an attribute of the divine. So when you are being kind, you are acting as a goddess or god yourself, working here on earth.

If only being kind was a simple matter—there are so many reasons to be. Kindness often requires that we give freely of our resources: time, energy, or perhaps even material resources as gifts. It's easy when you are almost guaranteed to get something in return, such as helping a customer in a service or retail job. It's tougher to be kind when there is no expectation of receiving a reward.

Kindness Exercise

The exercise for this virtue is to perform random acts of kindness. Random acts of kindness are fun because you can choose how you perform them and who you will surprise. However, they do require some creativity. Being mindful that your goal is to show compassion, this is a wonderful opportunity for you to practice proactive visualizations of how your actions will be kind and turn out best for the greatest good of all.

Start by thinking about times when you expect kindness in life. For example, you might expect the server at a restaurant to be kind to you when taking your order, even if you're being very picky about what you want. How would a server be kind?

You can expect a smile, patient listening, a warm voice, and anticipation of your needs. Now think of a situation in which you do not expect kindness. You probably don't expect kindness while doing everyday chores around the house, since cleaning up and taking care of bills is a pretty thankless job. What are some other times when kindness is unexpected in your life? Think about how you might be able to surprise someone with an act of kindness during those times in his or her life.

Next, think about what resources you have to give. If you have disposable income, paying for something is an excellent random act of kindness. You could take care of a random person's bill in a restaurant or add extra time to someone's parking meter, for example. If cash isn't a resource you have to spare, think about whether you can give your time or energy. For example, do a chore for someone, create a craft, or simply be extra sweet to someone with your words. Different people have different resources to share, so don't be ashamed if you don't have a lot of money or a lot of extra time and energy to spare. Give only the amount that keeps you feeling comfortable. Your act of kindness doesn't have to be a grandiose gesture. Experiment with even tiny acts of kindness to see what results you get. You may start a chain reaction of kindness in the world around you with even the simplest act.

Finally, choose somebody to receive your random act of kindness. You don't have to pick a stranger; you can perform a random act of kindness even for someone living in your home. Since our goal is compassion, you might choose somebody you may have harmed in some way. Your act of kindness may not be entirely random in this case, but consider it an opportunity to mitigate harm by offsetting it with kindness. If there's nobody you've harmed that needs reconciliation, you might choose somebody who is suffering for some other reason. In this way, you can reduce the harm of this suffering in the world by cheering that person up a little bit. You can perform your random act of kindness anonymously but it's not necessary. The point of this exercise is to mitigate harm with kind acts, nothing more and nothing less.

After you execute your random act of kindness, pay attention to how you feel. Notice if the person repaid you in any way, if only with sweetness and kindness in return. Even if the person did not repay you, did you felt good about what you did? The resulting goodness of performing random acts of kindness can help lift the burdens that you feel in life. Some people feel extremely uplifted by acts of altruism. In this way, kindness can help reduce one's own suffering, even if the suffering is just a lousy mood. If your random act of kindness affected you and others in a positive way overall, plan to do it again. You can set a day of the week as your random act of kindness day and make it part of your routine, or you can set specific reminders for yourself, like an alert on your calendar every payday. Over time, adding these kindness injections to your ordinary life can be like rays of sunshine burning away the fog of lassitude.

Sweetness

Though sweetness and kindness are often used interchangeably, in the context of what you're learning here I'm going to separate the virtue of sweetness so we can examine it with full attention. Sweetness is the manner by which you perform actions and say your words, so kindness and sweetness used together are ideal. Some people find it easier to do one or the other. Consider the case of the police officer assigned to give parking tickets. She can't afford to be kind enough to pay off everyone's tickets herself, but she can certainly afford to use a soft voice and an apologetic smile if she runs into somebody whose car she's ticketed. In the opposite case, my best friend's father has never been able to master sweetness, but he can do kindness. Whenever he's made a mistake and harmed her with rude words, he likes to give her a gift in order to make up for it, since he never learned from his family how to use his words sweetly in apology. These two examples of how sweetness and kindness can mitigate harm on their own hopefully shows you how they work best together. For now, let's continue to examine sweetness on its own, so that you can use it in your own life.

Sweetness is the manner of delivery of words and actions you use every day. Many people struggle to be sweet and honest at the same time. In my line of work as a fortune teller, being sweet while delivering bad news is tough work. In discussing the problem with colleagues who are also fortune tellers, the temptation we face is to sugar-coat news given to clients. However, in that case, the sweetness is not necessarily kind. The clients are paying us to deliver a message about the past, present, or future, and if we only tell them the good things, we may be shortchanging them. Worse still, if we lie in order to make the experience sweet, the person has been robbed of the truth entirely. Neither of these options are acceptable to me unless a client specifically asks to only hear the good stuff.

Luckily, there's a way to be sweet even in tough conversations without being dishonest. Here is some advice drawn from my years as a professional psychic I even use with my family and friends in everyday life. It draws a little bit from the "Martian" approach of problem-solving and the "Venusian" approach of using empathy, mentioned earlier. The trick is to use both of these approaches at the right time and be responsive to the emotional needs of the person to whom you are talking.

Begin with the empathetic approach while listening to the other person. If the person is upset, try to imagine feeling the way he or she is feeling in the moment. Then express your sympathy before speaking. One way to do this is to paraphrase what the person has told you to show you've been a good listener. Recall your active listening practice. You might say, "I'm sorry to hear about your dog; that must be devastating." Only after you've expressed some sympathy should you move on to any problem-solving approaches that you might use to lessen the harm and suffering that you see in front of you. You can phrase these as curious questions if you want, in order to continue the sweet tone of your message. For the preceding example, "I wonder, have you thought of adopting a new puppy?" These questions allow you to approach problem-solving in a sensitive way.

When I need to give clients bad news, I always try to phrase it in the form of empowering advice rather than flatly telling them their hopes aren't likely to come true or sugar-coating the truth by making it still seem possible. If a client is hurting after a breakup and is hoping that her ex will come back to her, I first offer my sympathy, and express that I'm sorry she's suffered such a loss. I ask her if she's ready for any answer, even if it is negative. I want to make sure she's not too vulnerable even to hear bad news delivered sweetly. Then, if it is my duty to tell her that her ex is not likely to come back, I offer problem-solving by inviting her to consider her potential with other partners.

Sweetness itself can't remove all of the world's harms and suffering, but it can easily soften the blow of rough news, or grease the wheels of human interaction, in order to make the world a better place. As practiced as I am with being sweet to my clients in a professional capacity, I do struggle with being sweet in everyday life with my family, who sees me at my worst.

In such cases, I end up having to give myself time to think before I respond if my emotions are getting the better of me.

If you find yourself challenged with a conversation in which it feels impossible to stay sweet, try stepping out of the conversation for a moment. Excuse yourself to the bathroom if you're at work, or perhaps be honest with your family member and tell him that you need a moment to cool down and will resume the conversation when you're ready. Then, ground yourself and shield yourself (the process is explained in chapter 3). Grounding will allow you to release some of your emotional upset, and shielding will prevent you from undue influence from the other person when you return to the conversation. Practice your words of sympathy and problem-solving if needed, take a deep breath, and return to the interaction when you're ready.

Sweetness Exercise

This exercise is practical, allowing you to spread sweetness into the world. You're going to write a sweet letter to someone who has helped you in your life or who has taught you about compassion. Think of this as writing a letter of thanks. Through my experience as a schoolteacher and as a mother, I found that these two vocations are often thankless jobs. Even when the children I've helped think fondly of me, it's a rare and precious gift for a teacher to receive a letter of thanks from a former student or for a mother to be thanked for a tough lesson she had to help her child learn.

For this exercise you could choose a parent, teacher, or anyone else in your life. Think about someone who may not receive sweet letters very often, because you might be able to brighten that person's day. Perhaps choose an elder who lives alone or someone who has a hard job helping people through tough times like a counselor or even a probation officer.

Once you have this person in mind, take a moment to think positive things about this person. Close your eyes and relive those moments with this special person that filled you with joy, wisdom, or love. Open your eyes and begin writing your letter of thanks. Be very specific about your thankfulness. For example, I wrote to one of my life teachers telling him about a day when I was feeling sad and disappointed with my health struggles, and he told me that spirit could overcome any disability. By writing about that specific moment in time, I was able to share that moment again with him by thanking him for it years later.

When you've finished writing your letter, send it off to the person in question. E-mail is fine, but handwritten letters have a sweet and personal touch. By extending your gratitude to others you'll find yourself remembering good moments in your life more frequently. You may also find that others are more generous with their sweetness toward you. A regular practice of gratitude can be an excellent way to become more mindful and compassionate.

Generosity

In the section of this chapter on kindness, I discussed a little bit about how you can only give a random act of kindness up to your ability and comfort level. I'd like to explore the virtue of generosity a little further in the context of reducing harm in the world because it is a sticking point for many people, myself included. If you're reading this, you may be one of the privileged people of the world since you've had enough resources to be able to achieve literacy and have time to read for pleasure. It's quite natural to feel guilty that there are other people on the world who don't share the wealth we have. That said, you're probably not the richest person in the world either. Wealth is limited by our surroundings and our needs. Money constantly flows in and out of our grasp. When you feel compassion for people who have next to nothing, generosity is one solution that comes to mind instantly.

Consider the case of the homeless. Walking down the street, you may see a lot of homeless people, most of them suffering the harms of hunger and exposure. If you reach in your pocket and find change, you can certainly give some to a homeless person. However, there's no guarantee that you will reduce that person's harm. In fact, having money to spend on drugs and alcohol could potentially increase the harm befalling a homeless person who happens to struggle with addiction. Above all, a gift is a gift. When being generous, you surrender your ability to direct those resources after you give them. Even if the money were guaranteed to reduce harm to the homeless, it can be a challenge to decide how much to give in order to maximize the use of your funds. There also comes a point when you must stop giving in order to prevent harm to yourself, your family, and anyone else who shares your money.

Ethics are like a puzzle with many parts. As with choosing random acts of kindness, I suggest working backward by first determining what you have in excess to share. For some, it may be money, but that would require a good look at their budgets first. If you've never written down your annual, monthly, weekly, and daily budget, please do so before choosing to give regularly. If you have no extra money to spare, consider giving of your time as service and volunteer work. And if you have no money or time, you still may have energy to give in prayer and meditation for a better world as well as in smiles and sweetness given to all.

You can also "budget" your time and energy by not signing yourself up for more activities than you can handle. Leave space in your calendar for new things, especially if you're proactively looking for new activities that harm none. Know when to call it quits on the recurring activities on your calendar that no longer serve you, especially if they're starting to actually harm your budget, sleep schedule, or social life. Be ruthless about cutting these harmful activities from your calendar, even if you think you'll disappoint someone. Use your sweet-talking skills to deliver the news in a kind way, and clear space to devote your resources to something more deserving and better aligned with your values.

You'll need to prioritize your time, money, and energy by taking a look at your deepest values and deciding which are most important. Create a list of issues that inspire passion in your heart. For example, your deepest values might be protecting the environment or protecting the freedoms of people. You might have a heart for social justice for a specific group of people, such as battered women, impoverished children, or the mentally ill. Think about which of these issues causes pervasive harm that you'd like to lessen in some way.

These may be issues of political import. It seems everyone has a hot button issue for which they cast their vote every time. For me, it all boils down to protecting the environment, as we need a healthy planet to safeguard our future. Without it, much of the life on earth could become extinct. For my husband, it comes down to protecting the rights guaranteed in the United States Constitution. He believes freedom is the essential issue. Without it, voting itself would become extinct. It's okay if your issue isn't political, however. It may be more personal and deal directly with relationships in your life. For example, if you lost a child to cancer, you'd probably want first and foremost to reduce the harm of pediatric cancer.

Generosity Exercise

Pick one issue that makes sense to you for this exercise, specifically about how you could best serve your most important issue with the resources you have. If you just have time or money to spare, the answer will be obvious. But if you have multiple means to combat the harmful issue, you can divide your efforts according to how much time and money you have in your budget. For example, you might find you can give twenty dollars and two volunteering days a month to your cause.

The next step is to decide how you will apply your resources. If you know somebody, even remotely, who is being harmed by this issue, pick that person first. If not, choose one of the potentially many organizations that have already dedicated themselves to your goal. Instead of reinventing the wheel, you may be able to join efforts with other passionate people and make your resources go further. Search carefully to find out which organization can use your resources the most effectively. If you're giving money, find out how much of their annual budget involves spending money directly on the cause to mitigate harm, as opposed to administrative and advertising costs. If you're volunteering with an organization, find out what positions are available that directly work to reduce the harms that concern you.

Also think about whether you want to work locally or globally. If you want to help malnourished children, would it feel better to you to give money to an organization that helps starving children overseas? Or would you prefer to donate to a soup kitchen or food bank in your neighborhood? If there are no organizations that are effectively working toward your goals, you may have to get creative. Think about how you can directly interact with harmed parties you want to help. That way, you can deliver sweetness and kindness as well as your donation of time or money. Think also about how you can help out the people with whom you already have relationships. It is one thing to donate to a pediatric cancer association, but quite another to visit a friend's child in the hospital when he's dealing with cancer.

Humility

Another common spiritual virtue, humility is closely associated with the spiritual injunction to be compassionate. Pride can be a barrier to reducing harm in several ways, namely that it can make one less cautious about harming others, and if a good deed is performed for reasons of pride, motivation dwindles when praise or other reward for the action does not follow.

There are two forms of motivation that get people to do things: intrinsic motivation, which arises from your internal self, and extrinsic motivation, where an external force such as money, social currency, or another reward comes to the individual. Extrinsic motivation fails as soon as the rewards stop coming, because it's disheartening to not be recognized for our efforts.

The best way to create a habit of reducing harm and living compassionately is to gently nurture our intrinsic motivation. To do this, examine your motives for choosing what you do when donating or doing volunteer work. You can sit in meditation and visualize your help doing good for the world, and see what happens afterward. Ask yourself if you would feel disappointed or sapped of motivation if you were not properly recognized for your good deeds. There's nothing wrong with being able to see good things happening and feeling good about it. Your good actions will be even more effective if you can commit to some longterm volunteer opportunities or donations. In the long run, motivation will have to become intrinsic, and so being humble is vital in the face of the world's needs.

Using humility in your relationships can also help them grow and reduce any harm that comes from prideful boasting or ignoring others' needs in favor of your own. Humble yourself in your marriage or family relationships and in your friendships. Pay attention to the times you feel you need an external reward in order to feel happy, such as if you feel hurt about not receiving a thank-you note after sending a gift to someone. Nurture your intrinsic motivation to love your friends and family and help them avoid the harms of harsh words or careless actions from you. Some spiritual people do this by giving all credit for good actions to the divine, to the point where even if one has achieved amazing things and not harmed any in the process, it is be important to thank higher powers; all the power a person has in life is on loan from the divine, including the power to be compassionate. Allow humility to give us the joyful perspective that we're serving a divine purpose here in the world. Expect from yourself nothing more and nothing less than expressing your purpose here on earth.

Secret Altruistic Gift Exercise

For this exercise, don't think you have to give a physical gift. You can also give a service or chore done by you as an altruistic act. The trick is that you must choose something to do in secret so you won't receive any thanks or reward for this action. I like brainstorming altruistic gift ideas; it makes me feel like a fairy godmother floating through the world and showering people with blessings.

Start by looking through your home for chores that are usually thankless duties. In my home, nobody notices if I clean the toilets, mop the floors, or even wash the car. Setting up these extra chores as secret gifts is one way I can motivate myself to do them out of love for my family rather than in the hopes that I'll receive praise for all the work I do around the house. You can also do similar chores out in the community. There may be a public garden that needs weeding, some sidewalks that need to be swept, or other tidying that needs doing. You could anonymously donate food to a food bank or clothes to a charity thrift store.

After you've chosen your altruistic gift and carried it out, here's a writing exercise you can do to boost your compassion and keep the positive energy from the experience moving in your life. Write your own quick letter of thanks addressed to yourself, rather than hoping for thanks from others. The way I do this is by writing a letter of thanks to my deities and placing it on my family altar. For example, if I spent the day helping a neighbor with some yardwork, I write down a note of thanks for the blessings of strong legs and a healthy back that give me the ability to help my community. I collect these brief notes counting my blessings in a notebook that stays near my family altar so I can add new ones every day if I wish. You can write notes of thanks to the divine, any higher power you worship, or simply to your higher self in your journal. This activity helps remind us that being able to give to others is a gift in and of itself. One day I may not be healthy or able enough to help others with physical chores, or wealthy enough to give food to those in need, so I do what I can when I can and give thanks.

Perfect Trust

I know I'm not alone when I recall the pain of having relationships in which trust was lacking. I remember being a teenager having to explain to my similarly-aged boyfriend why it was less compassionate to wait to break up with me until *after* he'd found a new love. A breakup and a betrayal was far more hurtful than a simple breakup would have been. You see, love and trust are interconnected; pledging to live compassionately is an act of trust and faith. It involves trusting that other people are going to try their best to support your goal, that some situations will create no accidental harm, and that, possibly, in the universe's higher powers, compassion is possible and necessary.

As in other faiths, spiritual seekers in my religious tradition must find a valid, practiced teacher or elder in order to become an apprentice to and learn the faith's ways and customs from. As an elder of this tradition, one of the tricky parts of meeting a new potential student is figuring out whether the person is trustworthy and whether he or she can trust me. If a student doesn't trust the teacher, then he or she will simply not be motivated to learn. It would be a waste of time if either one of us is untrustworthy. That's why we typically have a year and a day or more as a "getting to know you" period before committing to a student-teacher relationship.

Some people have problems with trust due to past abuse or some other trauma. If you suffer from a lack of ability to trust, it's not hopeless. Consider addressing the issue with the help of a qualified therapist. Trust is an important virtue and tool for anyone seeking to lead a compassionate life.

Nobody avoids being trustworthy. The vast majority of people want to think they are honest people and that others will be honest with them. We've been socially conditioned such that we know that untrustworthiness is bad, and that's a good thing! It means we've all been working on honesty since we were preschoolers. Having more trustworthy people in the world definitely means reducing harm. It pays to examine just how trustworthy you are, to add to the overall improvement of the world. It is unfortunate, therefore, that societal biases often destroy trust with class or race divisiveness. The fear and mistrust caused by racism and sexism are one reason why people seeking to live compassionately will fight these systems at every turn.

It is in your best interest to present yourself to the world in such a way that you are trustworthy while still being true to yourself. Get yourself certified in CPR and first aid, or consider training to be a volunteer lifeguard. If you're looking for a career that involves helping others, there are plenty of certifications, professional licenses, and degrees that can give you trustworthy credentials. Throughout life we all seek to gain respect from others. It is doubly important when living a compassionate lifestyle because gaining someone's trust and respect is necessary if you want to render aid. So don't take any shortcuts here. Although superficial changes such as dressing like a respectable person might help, it will take sincere lifelong dedication to your goals if you want to go the extra mile of making compassionate living part of your career choice. People trust with their hearts when they connect with you—and they also trust evidence.

Trust Exercise

Don't worry, I'm not going to suggest you perform the classic backward fall into a partner's arms. Trust falls are more of a physical strength and reaction time exercise than they are about actual trust. This is a solitary writing exercise; I know that trust doesn't come easily to everyone and that's okay. I already know that readers want to be more trustworthy. The tricky part is knowing how to open ourselves to the world as individuals worthy of trust. You can't simply put the word "honest" before your name—not without arousing suspicion! Instead, let's consider that certain "something" about trustworthy people and their kind and compassionate manner that draws others to their sides.

Let's make a brainstorming bubble chart to easily link ideas as you're thinking about them. Get a blank sheet of paper or turn to a page in your journal and write the word "trust" surrounded by a circle. Take a moment to close your eyes and think about somebody you have trusted in your life. Relive moments of trust in your mind and visualize how that person acted and carried himself or herself. Draw a line from that center bubble and write down some words and phrases you associate with that person's trustworthiness. For example, thinking about my trustworthy husband, I could write "shows his emotions clearly on his face," and "speaks up immediately when he has doubts." Recalling my trustworthy mother, I could write "kind, smiling face" and "always offers a helping hand." Writing about my best friend, I can write "reliable and punctual" as well as "gives me the benefit of the doubt." Circle each of these phrases to create their own bubbles.

Now you should have a little cluster of bubbles. They don't describe one trustworthy person but many. You should have some concrete ideas now about how to demonstrate your own trustworthiness. For example, giving people kind smiles like my mother does is one way I can show that I am trustworthy. If you need to, you can draw more branches to make your ideas more concrete. For example, if I want to give people the benefit of the doubt like my best friend does for me, I could write down "wait and listen when people speak, refraining from judgment." You can use this bubble brainstorming technique with people you love as examples for any virtue under the sun.

Silence

The ability to keep silent is a virtue. Recall the common advice from mothers everywhere: "If you don't have anything nice to say, don't say anything at all." This essential rule of compassion was something I learned as a preschooler, probably so that I and my classmates would stop calling others mean names. I'm now teaching my young children the same thing, and I admit it's still very difficult for me to hold my tongue! In our age of social media, it's easier than ever to hurt someone's feelings with a careless remark or alienate others due to differences of creed or politics. The word "silence" takes on new meaning in relation to instant forms of communication, extended to include a lack of response to a provocative message. Silence is my main tool when I try to refrain from vain and foolish conversation.

You may find it easier to remain silent instead of arguing or insulting someone when the person isn't an anonymous stranger. Perhaps it is easiest for you when you face a friend or family member right in front of you because you don't want to harm him or her. Maybe it's actually harder in those cases, because you have friendly rivalry built into your relationships with some friends and family members. The latter situation can be problematic when your friend or loved one is feeling particularly vulnerable and emotional. Real hurt feelings can result even from simple jokes.

Consider changing the relationship somewhat by being gentler with each other and refrain from taking opportunities to make jokes at another's expense. It might sound awkward, but it is possible. I've done this with my husband and also with one of my friends with whom I used to have a relationship based on giving each other a hard time. You might feel like you're being a spoilsport, but you'll find that the fun of joshing your friends or family can be replaced with a different feeling of camaraderie in which you are comfortable to share even your deepest fears and hopes.

Gates of Speech Exercise

I'll let you in on a prayer I recite every morning in the shower as I prepare for my day. I try to allow myself to slip into a meditative mindset. This is pretty easy for me early in the morning when I'm still half asleep and my brain is settled into an alpha wave state. If you want to use this prayer at a different time of day, that's fine too. Just try to give yourself some alone time so you can make the commitment to yourself.

The prayer is from a Sanskrit saying of indeterminate origin, and it goes like this:

> Let no words pass my lips this day
> unless they first pass these three gates of speech:
> Is it true? Is it necessary? Is it kind?

Another helpful exercise is meditating on each of these three gates of speech. Try seating yourself in meditation and visualizing a happy place that makes you feel safe from harm. Visualize three doors. On the first is written "Is it true?" On the second you see the words, "Is it necessary?" And on the third, you see the question "Is it kind?" Think about which door you'd like to open to see what that particular virtue looks like in action. Know that beyond each door lies the perfect example of the virtue in question. Once you've chosen a door, open it and peek inside to see what's going on.

What do you see in your mind's eye? What does the landscape look like? What objects appear? Do you see other people, animals, or other characters? How are they interacting with one another? What does their body language look like to you? Can you make out any words they might be saying to one another? Now step through the door. Do any of the individuals in your vision acknowledge you? If so, what do they say to you?

Now imagine that one of them hands you an object. What is it? When you're ready, turn around and walk back through the door to your safe and happy place. If you feel ready to go through a new door, try another one. Or, you can save the other doors for meditation on another day if this exercise was profound and overwhelming for you.

A common modern interpretation of this Sanskrit saying is to use the mnemonic "THINK" in the following way:

- T = Is it true?

- H = Is it helpful?

- I = Is it inspiring?

- N = Is it necessary?

- K = Is it kind?

I find that this modern interpretation is a little overwhelming; after all, I'm not trying to get rid of *all* meaningless conversations forever. There's still value to me in chit-chatting about the weather with new acquaintances or joking about nonsense with my kids. Even though I am a spiritual teacher, most of the things I actually say are far from inspiring. For the purposes of living with compassion, I like to keep my speech in accordance with the simple three: truth, necessity, and kindness. Truth helps build my trustworthiness for others. Necessity reminds me that sometimes remaining silent is a virtue. Silly jokes can also be necessary to maintain a relationship, and that's okay. The truly unnecessary speech is whatever takes away from my ability to truly listen to others. And finally, we've already discussed how kindness is a divine virtue that can make someone's day.

Mirth

They say that laughter is the best medicine. Mirth is joy and amusement at the comedy that is life. It's vital for anyone interested in compassionate living for many reasons, but namely to avoid becoming a stick in the mud, depressed by the potential for harm that lurks everywhere. Mirth can be an injection of joy that salves the soul. Some even promote laughter as therapy, faking loud and boisterous laughter until it dissolves into real giggles.

Laughter can be important for yourself as well as others. For your own benefit, laughing at yourself can reduce perceived harm immensely. If a friend is poking fun at you, for example, playing along can feel like one way to maintain the friendship and also find humility within yourself. This doesn't mean that you have to play the part of the doormat and let people make you the butt of their jokes all the time; this is about changing your own attitude so you can find amusement in unfortunate situations of your own. Diffuse uncomfortable situations with laughter.

You'll often find that in the moment something does not seem funny, but then when you look at it from the perspective of some point in the future, it is actually amusing and not a big deal. This is particularly true of childhood foibles. Think now about some funny stories from your younger years that might have been distressing at the time. Perhaps you have childhood memories of minor cases of embarrassment, fear, and anger or sadness—revisit them now with an adult's perspective. Off the top of my head, I can think of stories of panicking when my first tooth fell out, the embarrassment of wetting my pants in preschool, feeling enraged about getting a shot at the doctor, and feeling overwhelming sadness about not having cable television. As a grown woman, these minor events that produced big feelings for a small child seem amusing to me. After you've thought of some stories of your own, consider how many of your current troubles may seem amusing in ten years or more. Since much of my day involves the circus that is caring for small children, I feel a lot of anger, sadness, fear, and embarrassment that I believe will also be funny for me in a few years. Try stepping outside of yourself to diffuse the harm you feel now. Remember this Ralph Waldo Emerson quote: "Keep cool. It will all be one a hundred years hence."

Mirth Exercise

When I was a kid, I wrote down jokes in a little notebook I carried around. My notebook of jokes wasn't for any grand purpose or any plans to be a comedy writer; I don't think I even knew what stand-up comedy was at the time. What I did know was that some jokes seemed funny in the moment but when I looked back on them later on, the mirth of the moment had faded. The idea of enduring joy has always fascinated me, like being able to bottle a smile for later as a useful magical skill, indeed. As I grew older, the practice of writing down funny jokes became more difficult. I started to overthink things instead of using the observational comedy that came naturally to me when younger. Observing mirthful moments is still very valuable to me, and it can be an important part of self-compassion. For this exercise, I'd like you to start a little notebook that will become at least a hundred mirthful moments you can pull out and review whenever you're feeling blue.

The key to observational comedy is to be observant and write down your observations the moment they happen. You'll of course need some paper and a writing implement that can travel with you. I use a tiny memo notebook that came with a matching pen. In a pinch, you could even use a piece of folded printer paper and a golf pencil stuffed in your back pocket. When you notice a mirthful moment, write it down. When my two-year-old son said that he had been tired for a hundred million years I wrote it down. When my daughter chased some chickens while asking them why they didn't want to be her friend, I wrote it down. Whenever my husband comes out with a one-liner or my mother tells me about a silly dream, I write it down. These moments I carry with me in my pocket. Try it yourself, and then take out your notebook later and read over it. You may find that the humor that existed in some of those moments faded with time, and that's okay. Other written memories might bring back those moments in your mind and make you smile. Still others may have a timeless humor you can even share with others.

Merry Meet and Merry Part

In another line of Gwen Thompson's poem about compassionate life, she writes, "Merry meet and merry part, bright the cheeks and warm the heart." Much like the line quoted earlier, a picture of a good listener is painted. This phrase about greetings and partings shows how to be proactive about sweetness and kindness. Acts of kindness are like windows of healing to which people who are hurting can turn. The week of this writing, I was involved in a nasty car accident from which my children and I walked away with only scrapes and bruises. A truck crossed the center line and hit my car head on. The aftermath of the accident was terrifying. There were moments of wondering whether anyone was injured, and hours of dealing with paramedics, firefighters, and police as the road was cleared of the two vehicles. My neighbor showed up on the scene and the moment of being greeted by a friendly face felt like a miracle. He allowed my kids to sit in his warm car, away from the devastation, and asked if there was anything else he could do for us when we parted. When we finally reached home, safe and sound, my daughter said, "It was very nice how the man let us sit in his car. That was an act of kindness!"

We don't always get the opportunity to be the hero who saves the day during a tragedy, but there's something important about greetings and partings in every culture. It is so important that some companies pay people to take jobs as greeters, where they simply greet and bid goodbye to everyone who walks into or out of the business. We're taught to greet guests at the door of our homes and see them to the door when they leave. Each culture has a script of words that we say, such as, "I had a lovely time, thanks for having me." If these niceties are omitted by either party, the hosts might feel angry and the guests might feel unwelcome.

There is magic in these simple actions that can help us become compassionate creatures. They act as the beginnings and endings of the rituals of conversation in our culture. They can be cues to remind us to act with sweetness and kindness in any situation. Asking the simple greeting question, "How are you?" gives a chance for someone to open up and share potential sources of harm in their lives so we may be able to offer sympathy or problem-solving. Many of us brush off this question with a standard answer even when we're not doing very well at all. It may do you good to pay attention to how you answer that question for others, to allow them opportunities to help. Think about how you greet the people you see each day. Find a way to make your routine greetings more sweet and kind.

Greeting and Parting Exercise

This writing exercise is a way to write out how you'd like to welcome and bid farewell to the people in your life. I first started being intentional about how I said goodbye to people after a series of events led me to think about how important this was. Firstly, my father died, which made me think about all of the times I said goodbye to him in my life. As a child it was, "See you later, alligator," followed by, "After a while, crocodile." As an adult he'd give me a funny little salute that he still gives me in my dreams.

Shortly after his death, I went back to school for Clinical Pastoral Education to be a hospital chaplain. We had really bonded as students and teachers by the time we reached the end of our time together. My supervising chaplain asked us to think about how we'd like to say goodbye. She said that some people were gift-givers who liked to hand out mementos when saying goodbye. Some people give emotional goodbyes with tears or hugs. Some people even like to start arguments with people just before leaving and storm off righteously instead of having to be sad when it's time to go. My kids went through a phase as toddlers during which they refused to hug their grandmother goodbye out of the childish hope that it would delay her departure. And some like to disappear off into the sunset. My supervisor called those who like to run away without making a big deal out of goodbyes the "Hi-ho, Silver" people, after the Lone Ranger's famous parting cry. As a joke, when I left after receiving my certificate, I yelled "Hi-ho, Silver!" and ran out the door. But afterward, I started wondering if I really wanted to always be the one to slip out the side door before the end of meetings, or if I wanted to truly connect with people like the loved ones in my life did and still do.

Start by thinking about how you tend to greet people now. It's okay if you're shy or you avoid the whole process like I used to do, routinely, with quick and perfunctory greetings. Next think about how you'd like to connect with people when you greet them. Write down your ideal greeting. For example, perhaps you'd like to look the person in the eye, smile, shake his or her hand, and use his or her name when saying hello. Doing this helps you connect with the person's humanity and helps you remember names. Perhaps you'd like to share a spiritual greeting like "Namaste" to recognize that the spirit in others is the same that lives within you. Write down your idealized greeting. Visualize yourself greeting people in this way as if it were a reality. Try it out the next time you meet someone, even if it's the check-out clerk at the grocery store.

Now think about how you tend to say your goodbyes. If your natural inclination is to run out the door with a "Hi-ho Silver" that's okay. If you want, you can change your automatic goodbyes. Now, I choose to tell my children at night and when I drop them off at school, "Merry meet, merry part, and merry meet again." I chose my parting phrase from my faith tradition to emphasize that I will greet them just as happily when I see them again. Perhaps you'd like to choose a parting phrase that expresses your love. I will always treasure the fact that my last words my father and I spoke to each other before he died were "I love you." I try my best not to take any goodbyes for granted anymore.

two

Find Your Life's Purpose

Hopefully you've been able to start some new routines and strategies in your life to bring more compassion into your relationships and to focus on the physical well-being of others. Now we'll move to the reasoning behind the fact that so many religious faith traditions ask us to be kind. If you are a part of a particular religion, perhaps a clergy member can direct you toward the prayers, scripture, or spoken lore that encourages consideration for others. If you have an eclectic spiritual practice free of labels, perhaps your own practices can draw strength from the rich traditions that stand united on this issue.

One thing about humanity that consistently amazes me is how some archetype or ideal like the Golden Rule can arise in many different places and cultures simultaneously. It could be that such an idea originated in one place and spread. But before modern travel, it may be more likely that there is something special about the human condition that led many people separately to the same conclusion. It's almost as if humanity possesses a collective deep memory or a sort of hive mind. Going on that assumption, I'll use this chapter to help you plug in to these shared truths. Remember, though, that you don't necessarily need my help or really the help of any other person—this reality has been with you from the very beginning.

Before continuing, it may be helpful to remember when you were first inspired by the idea of compassionate living. It may have been learned from a wise grandparent or a sacred book. It might have been discovered independently when you decided as a child to spare an ant's life rather than frying it under a magnifying glass. Close your eyes and try to recreate a moment in your mind when the lesson of compassion as key seemed true. There is some reason that made compassion a sacred truth for you. It might have been an intellectual reasoning in your mind or simply a feeling in your bones. Revive this motivation and continue in your quest.

Ethics

Before we delve into ethics, it's important to review the semantics and the difference between morals and ethics. Morals tell you what is good and what is bad, and ethics are edicts that tell you what you should or should not do in society. We know that murder is wrong; that's a moral judgment. We also know that you should not hit somebody when angry—ethics tell us this behavior is poor. Often, ethics are thought to be handed down from a higher power. In any case, it helps to know the difference between morals—self-determined—and ethics— determined by others. In this way you can discover the true source of your sense of right and wrong. It is important to do this because humans are social animals and there are subtle exterior pressures that can work on our psychology and really affect whether we harm others.

The famous Milgram experiment, taught to many horrified first-year psychology students, is a good example. Random subjects were selected and told they would be delivering painful electric shocks to a person in the next room whenever that person gave a wrong answer on a simple quiz. The subjects were given a signal to inflict the shock and informed of the intensity of that shock by a very important-looking researcher. Unbeknownst to these research subjects, the person in the other room was not hooked up to any electricity and was actually not experiencing any pain whatsoever. Instead, there was an actor in the other room who would give dramatic yelps of pain.

The subjects proceeded with the experiment and delivered the supposed painful punishments as instructed, even when the yelps and screams became louder and sounded increasingly tortured. As the shocks' "voltage" was increased, the screams became desperate and then stopped entirely, as if the person in pain had lost consciousness or even died. The research subjects still delivered shocks as instructed. These were just ordinary people, but they thought they were doing something they should do, even though it would be incredibly harmful, because they were following the orders of somebody who spoke authoritatively and appeared to be in charge.

Though controversial, the experiment proves something about how the mind can explain away feelings in our conscience when we harm people. When I first heard about the Milgram experiment, I thought there would be no way I would have obeyed the orders to continue hurting people. However, the subjects in the experiment were steeped in the situation. The important-looking researchers really seemed like they knew what they were doing. In life, I often follow the ethical lead of people that I respect and admire, and I rarely make important decisions without first consulting with people I believe know more than me. As a result, I have to be explicit with myself about my own morals and ethics before talking to others.

Ethics can change according to the situation, sometimes drastically. It's easy to come up with ethical conundrums, whereas morals seem more simple. For now, let's take a look at the source of your morals and ethics regarding a harm-free lifestyle. Both of these usually come from your family, culture, and society at large. They were taught to you directly by others and indirectly through your experiences and subjective judgments. You know when you're acting morally and within the realm of ethics by how you feel as well as how others react to your actions. We'll look at some safety measures you can take to fortify your own moral and ethical behavior by consulting with your inner self.

You've already decided that harming yourself and others is generally bad. Other things that fit into that category would be murder and serious injury, so those are also both easily categorized as really bad things. Perhaps you remember the origins of learning these lessons. You might remember a church lesson about the commandment "Thou shalt not kill." Or you might remember your parents explaining to you that somebody who died in a movie was not really killed because killing people is wrong. Some other sorts of harm may be a little morally ambivalent. Is it wrong to break someone's heart in a relationship? If you learned this lesson, it was either taught to you by a parent or a friend or learned the hard way by experiencing the pain of heartbreak yourself.

Now, think about the ethical "should" and "should not" ideas you may have received in our society. You know, for instance, that you should drive carefully and have liability insurance on your car to prevent needless suffering in the case of a road accident. A good clue that something is unethical is when you ask yourself, "Is this legal?" or "Is this against the community rules?" Think about where you've learned ethical rules. Many of them may have been learned from parents, schoolteachers, and other authorities. If you have a job that could potentially cause physical or legal harm, you may have been taught specific procedures and regulations for your line of work that protect others from harm or misdeeds. For example, those who work with finances may have to follow rules such as always having more than one person sign a company check so there's no temptation to act unethically and write checks for a single person's individual financial gain. Again, these lessons are often taught by people in the organization who are in the know. It might not occur to a generally well-meaning individual to follow those rules and regulations otherwise.

Writing Your Own Statement of Ethics

I'm big on writing my own statements of ethics on a regular basis probably because I'm a business owner, and in the business of being an independent fortune teller, there's not a whole lot of industry oversight. Other than basic state and city licensure and certification to give advice for money, I'm on my own with clients once the door to my office closes. I take my interaction with clients as a huge responsibility since they respect what I have to say. There are likely very many people in your life who take what you have to say very seriously as well. Every word you speak can affect those around you. I post my personal statement of ethics prominently due to my role as a business owner, but you can write your statement of ethics in a private journal and keep it to yourself, if you like. The idea behind this exercise is to keep others in mind when you think about what you should and should not do.

It can help to write a statement of ethics if you first choose a context. In my example here, the context is my business relationship with clients. You can write a personal statement of ethics for your workplace, school work, pet care, volunteer work maintaining trails in the forest, or whatever else you like. The idea is to narrow your focus to make this exercise work for you.

Next, write down three "shoulds" and three "should nots." When I'm doing fortune-telling work, I should always tell the truth or keep silent. I should not perform fortune telling for children aged under eighteen unless I have permission from a parent or guardian. Write down some of your own rules for yourself in your own personal context of choice. Don't get bogged down in an excess of rules; limit yourself to just a few to focus on right now, and review your personal code of ethics later down the road. The ones that are easy for you to remember can become a part of your routine, and you can add more to the list that challenge you in the moment.

Virtues

Throughout these pages I've been naming some specific virtues common to many religions, such as the virtue of compassion. There are more virtues that may be missing from the list but are dear to your heart. Some are taught by some cultures and religious faith traditions but not others. For example, my religion values strength, beauty, and youth. Other faith traditions teach virtues that conflict with these. In fact, it may be challenging to find virtues among two people that align. Virtues are so highly personal that one person's fault may be another person's virtue. Some of my greatest virtues are also my greatest faults. I find that when I think about what drives me crazy about somebody I love, it's usually the same thing that made me fall in love with that person.

Now it's time to write down some virtues of your own. These don't necessarily have to be virtues that you have, but it's good to start with some you already demonstrate well. Once you've written those down, try writing down some virtues that you wish you had. Add to this list some virtues you admire in people you know. Finally, write down any virtues you value that may have been taught to you by spiritual teachers, schools, or other social organizations.

Hopefully you have a good list that is encouraging to you. Circle virtues that you believe can support your ability to live compassionately. For example, if patience is on your list, it can certainly help to you be more careful when driving or doing anything else that might cause harm when hastily done. Be imaginative and picture each virtue being acted out in many ways. Perhaps it will help to imagine people you know who embody those virtues. Now would be a good time to compliment some of the people you know for being especially exemplary models of those virtues. You might even get some tips as to how those people in your life came to be able to do so well at being virtuous.

Virtues Exercise

Here's a meditative exercise you can do to try becoming more virtuous. Pick one of the virtues you circled for this meditation. It can be tempting to pick several related virtues, but you should be gentle with yourself and not overwhelm yourself with too many expectations to live up to at once. If you're feeling ambitious, you can pick another virtue in a month's time. A very good time to do this meditation would be during the full moon, as the moon's fullness represents the virtue ripening, filling out, or coming to full term within you. At the following full moon, you can choose a different virtue or repeat the exercise with the same virtue if it still needs work. I have a spiritual teacher who prays every day to be punctual, and she's still working on that one because she's chronically late to everything. In the same way, I repeatedly work on my three gates of speech. There's no shame in not being perfect.

Once you have your chosen virtue and before you start meditating about it, brainstorm some visual ideas for what that virtue would look like if it was applied in your life. One way to do this is to create a vision board, a collage of images that depict things you want to draw into your life. Through the law of attraction, the more you focus on this board and its images, the more likely those things will appear in your life. Your vision board will be one way you can overlay these virtues on your self-image until they manifest.

Flip through old magazines for images that represent this virtue to you. You can also sketch your own images or search for and print out images from the Internet. Collect them all together on your vision board. Paste them together to make a collage, if you like. Place the vision board somewhere prominent, where you will see it every day. For your meditation, make sure to get your vision board and have it in front of you. If you're an especially visual and imaginative person, you may be able to construct a vision board entirely within your own head. For most of us, however, the physically constructed vision board is a powerful tool that helps you boost your signal in the universe.

When you sit down to meditate, first take a few minutes to close your eyes and clear your mind of distractions. You can set a timer for five or ten minutes, or you can just wait for cues from your body and mind that you're relaxed and not focused on external problems or activities. Ground yourself (instructions are in chapter 3), then open your eyes to look at your vision board. Let your eyes wander across the images associated with your virtue of choice. Close your eyes again.

This time, visualize yourself being virtuous and being the perfect example of this virtue. This is a time when it is appropriate to aim for perfection. Because you're trying to bring this virtue into your life, you want to visualize yourself as having already achieved your goal. That way, you'll draw that energy into your life. Avoid picturing yourself practicing and working toward your goal; in your imagination, you've *already* reached perfection. By doing so, you overlay the virtue on your own self-image. Hold this imagery in your mind for a few more minutes or as long as you can, and then relax. Ground yourself again. If you find that you're mentally or physically tired after this exercise, focus more on your grounding practice. Remember to place your vision board where you will see it frequently. You don't have to meditate or do anything special every time you look at it; simply let it work its magic in your life.

Karma

A discussion on how harming others affects the soul would not be complete without a mention of karma. Karma is the effect of good or bad deeds on the soul. There are two basic schools of thought about karma; the Eastern school of thought is historically the earlier of the two. No matter the school from which it originated, karma can be thought of like a currency spent throughout existence. It is *not* judgment dealt by some unseen or cosmic critic.

According to the Eastern school of thought, karma comes to the individual from deeds that tie you to the world, as well as the result of actions in past lives. Good and bad deeds pay out with karma. The goal of some Eastern religions is actually to rid oneself of karma entirely, the reason being release from the mundane into the divine. Releasing karma may require detaching oneself from the world, and indeed some monks and gurus spend their life as ascetics, hermits, or spiritual pilgrims. That same quest also can fit into an ordinary life through meditation and prayer. People who ascribe to the Eastern form of karma often believe reincarnation's goal is escaping the cycle of death and rebirth.

By contrast, the Western school of thought divides good karma and bad karma into a dichotomy of opposing luck where a person tries to acquire good karma through good deeds and avoids accumulating bad karma through bad deeds. Often the perceived mechanism for this sort of karma is the law of attraction. Recall that like attracts like, so good deeds therefore attract good luck in life, whereas a life of dastardly deeds would snowball into catastrophe either in this lifetime or in one to follow. Believers in reincarnation and the Western form of karma may or may not wish to escape the cycle of death and rebirth.

Consequently, some believe they will continue to be reborn, forever learning lessons in a constant flux of karma.

For simplicity's sake I made these two karmic systems seem very cut and dried, but in reality individuals who subscribe to a belief in karma may mix and match among the two, and each system of karma is informed with rich and varied religious traditions. You don't have to belong to a specific religion to believe in karma, but if you do it may be rewarding to study further within your own faith traditions.

Ultimately, all understandings of karma emphasize personal responsibility. Karma is meted out based on one's actions almost universally, like a law of physics. It takes no special wishing or efforts from you to set karma into motion, and indeed there may be no way to stop karma until it runs its proper course, balancing whatever mysterious forces our universe holds. It's a concept I find both unnerving and comforting. If somebody causes harm even when I fail to prevent that harm, justice can be provided by some impartial force external to me, releasing me from any duty to cause punishing harm out of my own sense of revenge. In this way, my own belief in karma can support my efforts to be kind.

The Threefold Law

Some people believe in a specialized form of karmic retribution called the rule of three or the threefold law. In this view of the karmic system, karma is not just balanced evenly, but is multiplied. As Gwen Thompson wrote in her poem, "Mind the threefold law you should, three times bad and three times good." The implication is that if you do good deeds, the good will come back to you multiplied three times. Likewise, if you do bad deeds, the bad will come back to you multiplied by three. This rule acts as an extra incentive to live with compassion and not inflict harm on anyone. If we imagine ordinary karma in the Western system to be a sort of teeter totter of justice, you push down on one end and the other end will go up; there is no escaping the fairness of this system, and it goes back and forth balancing out justice as it goes. The threefold law, on the other hand, has more of a snowball effect. If you roll a snowball down a hill, it gathers speed and packs snow until it is larger and can have a bigger effect.

If every harm that one did to another was immediately returned threefold, certainly no smart person would ever try to harm anyone ever. It's obvious that the threefold law many people find strength and inspiration in is more subtly applied. When I was first taught about the threefold law as a teenager, it sounded like something made up to scare a child. But the threefold can be understood as working with universal laws we already know. Consider that the threefold return can happen to the three spheres of body, mind, and spirit.

For example, imagine a thief. If karma worked like a fairy tale and he stole a stereo from a store, his own home would be burglarized or perhaps he would fall down the stairs and suffer injuries that cost as much as the stereo. But we all know the world doesn't always mete out justice so neatly. Instead, we know that stealing is wrong because we pay for it in other ways. Karma might work by allowing the thief to be caught, or theft may cause costs at the store to rise so the thief and people the thief cares about now have to pay more money for things that can't be stolen. These are financial problems that affect the thief's body. Mentally, the thief can be affected by knowing that he can't be trusted and that perhaps he can't trust anyone else. Spiritually, the thief may be affected by being tied to this bad karma. In this way, the threefold law can be understood as three fingers of justice that wrap around the thief, multiplying his problems in different ways.

Of course, those who believe in the threefold law often have stories to share about when the rule of three applied itself more literally or even multiplied itself several times more than just three. When I was a young teenager, I tried to cast a spell on someone who was a little too controlling, not respecting that person's free will. My father and I were arguing more and more, so I cast a spell to try to prevent him from arguing with me just for a few days. I was hoping the spell would temporarily turn him into the perfect dad who would let me do whatever I wanted. Well, it didn't work on him at all. It turns out that angry thirteen-year-old kids aren't always the best magicians. Instead, I got laryngitis and lost my voice for a week or so. At the time, I thought the rule of three was coming back to me for a longer time than I'd ever intended the controlling spell to work on my dad. I suppose it wasn't a total bust, though—I was in no shape to argue with him until I got well!

Will

Free will is an important part of many religious teachings; it is vital to understand its role when trying to live a compassionate lifestyle. I'm sure we all know somebody with self-destructive tendencies, like a friend or relative who struggles with addiction. You could lock that person up so he or she could never be harmed or tempted again, but that's not kind and it won't let that person have a good life. Would you choose to never leave your bed to prevent accidental harm? Controlling people to prevent harm is destructive in its own insidious way, because it causes harm to the mind and spirit of the people being oppressed.

What does it mean to truly "will" something to happen? Spiritually speaking, the will is the compelling force from within that draws a person toward destiny. This will is greater than mere desire. If you truly will for something to occur, magic happens—the world seems to bend itself to your will because nothing can stop you. When mythologist and philosopher

Joseph Campbell famously said to follow your bliss, he was talking about a person's true will. When you are aligned with your soul's true will and you're on the path of your destiny, even hardships will seem easy.

Think of a person who is truly happy with his or her vocation: the mother who lovingly soothes her baby in a stressful situation instead of going bonkers, the sandwich maker who joyfully serves up his craft day to day and can make substitutions and special orders seemingly without effort, the train conductor who commutes long hours through snowy mountains away from his family but finds peace within. These people are content with their surroundings not because the jobs are easy but perhaps because the people performing them will themselves to be happy with their chosen lot in life.

Teasing apart one's true will and one's desire is a tall order. On any given day, we are inundated with desires from within and also those caused by external pressure. Even highly spiritual people feel confused by desire, and those who seek to free themselves from good and bad karma entirely also seek to rid themselves of desire. Most troublesome of all, we sometimes desire to harm others or desire things that are self-destructive.

Sometimes one's true will is easier to see from the outside. Your family might know that you can be a wonderful aunt or a devoted nurse, but your desires tell you that all you want is for an ex-boyfriend to come back. It can be tricky to stay on track.

Just remember that listening to external sources can be helpful. This is why some of us have trusted parents or best friends on the other end of the phone at all hours during times of confusion and trouble. Someone outside your situation may see that circumstances are temporary.

Beyond external help, there are ways to understand your inner messages. Look at your situation as if you were another person. This sense of perspective helps you figure out which messages are desire and which are will. For example, in the heat of a breakup or in the months following the birth of a child, the calamity that is life may seem interminable. It's easy to make rash decisions that are not in accordance with our true will. That's why we shouldn't make big decisions after a major life change or loss.

Another way to understand true will is to compare notes with your spiritual beliefs or religious teachings. In the context of compassion, you could ask yourself if the divine would lead you to a particular action for the greatest good of all. Some say that desires which tell you to hurt someone are not "of God," using these inner questions about true will as the logic behind actions. No matter how supernatural or insistent the message may seem that is floating through your head, it is originating from your own brain and can safely be discarded or dealt with, as it is not of divine origin.

Don't let desires that are long lasting be confused with will. For example, in my work as a fortune teller I often see people who have trapped themselves in harmful relationships for very long periods of time—years and even decades. Both people in the relationship might be emotionally harmful to one another. In some cases, one or both partners make sacrifices of financial and physical health out of a desire to preserve the relationship. In these cases, the harm is clear to both people, yet the burden is not made light by love, spiritual bliss, or a sense of true will being followed. In fact, out of the intuition that true will is being distracted and diverted by the toxic relationship, resentment might build instead. When the breakup inevitably happens, there is of course a sadness for the loss. There is also a sense of relief that arrives with time, due to the ability to once again get back on track with one's true will. Some people are lucky enough to start working on their life's work in childhood, but many people make huge spiritual discoveries and life changes when middle-aged and even later.

Will Exercise

Think now about what you might truly will in life right now. Examine your strongest desires. Think about what you'd give anything to have or protect. Those desires may or may not be in accordance with your will. Write them down, circling the ones you think will harm none if carried out properly.

Next think about what things you truly will in life that you might already be carrying out successfully. You can ask close friends and family if you need help with some of these, as they may already be able to compliment some things that you seem born to do. They might also be able to give you some feedback on your heart's desires if you're willing and ready to receive such feedback. Write these things down and circle the ones you are successfully doing without causing harm.

If you proactively look for compassionate actions to do, that process has probably made your calendar pretty full. Now that you've written down some things that might be your true will, you may have some perspective on what things in your life deserve the most attention. Remember that even if something is your true will, it doesn't mean that it has to be your obsession. I believe that my spiritual path is my true will but I have a life outside of prayer and my ritual duties. Seeking balance is important, and you must always be moving in the direction of your true will with harm to none in the process.

Power

We all want to be empowered. Powerful people are in control of their lives; they're turning the steering wheel in the car on the road of life. Powerful people are not controlled by others, so they can't be forced to do harm that they would not wish to do. Power is not black and white, however. It can be wielded with gentle authority, like that of a loving parent. It can be balanced equally among peers, or it can be tipped out of balance in any relationship. When you have power over someone, it means you can get him or her to do something that he or she otherwise would not do. Giving a toddler a piece of candy for cleaning her room is a source of power. Scolding a dog while wielding a rolled up newspaper to keep it from chewing up shoes is another source of power.

Not all power is inherently harmful; it is okay to continue seeking power in your relationships, career, and even in a hierarchy within your spiritual groups. There's also such a thing as personal power—your ability to have control over your own desires, thoughts, and emotions. This power is perhaps the most valuable of all, and it is certainly vital if you're trying to live compassionately.

There are many ways to gain personal power, and I'd like to speak to spiritual means of harmlessly gaining power. Before that, it's important to note that there may be some mental barriers to being a powerful person. Psychological problems such as low self-esteem can prevent you from properly gaining or wielding personal power. Mental illnesses such as depression or post-traumatic stress disorder can also sap a sense of personal power in many situations. If you have any mental barriers to gaining personal power, know that it is not your fault. Actually, you empower yourself by reaching out for help if and when you need assistance. Working with your doctor and finding a trusted therapist can help you identify the areas in your life where you feel helpless against harm, and you can ultimately learn the skills to cope with mental challenges to your power.

Spiritually, many derive personal power directly from divinity. Some people do this by praying for what they desire. In chapter 4 is an example prayer for serious wishes and silly wishes for a loved one. If your will is in accordance with divine will, the wish will be granted and it is as if you have the power of a deity. If, however, the wish is against divine will (that is, harmful to the person in some way), the wish will not be granted. The power remains with deity, but it is acting through you. This may not seem like true power, but all power is actually relational and circumstantial, so it is just as real as the power of a presidency or the power love has to hold two people in a marriage.

Some believe the divine source of love in the universe is what gives people the inkling to pray. For example, one day I was walking in the grocery store and suddenly thought of a friend I hadn't seen in a while. She usually came to a weekly meditation gathering at my house but hadn't attended in a while due to family troubles. I felt a brief feeling of compassion and even worry for her, and I wondered whether I should say a quick prayer for her. If that thought was divinely inspired, then yes. In such a situation, my source of divine inspiration and I would have a sort of symbiotic relationship: my gods need me to pray, and

I need them to be a source of power. This may be an unusual way of looking at the divine for readers who believe in an omnipotent god, but remember that we all know we have personal power that plays a role in the universe. Even if an omnipotent god doesn't want murder to happen, it still does because people choose to do that harmful act. Likewise, if a higher power wants you to live compassionately, you're going to have to do your part practically and spiritually.

The prayer list of someone who wants to find a path to compassion can be comprised of obligatory prayers if that person chooses to make it a part of a spiritual duty. When somebody comes into your mind for prayer, write down that person's name and perhaps an inkling of what he or she might need. You might know because the person told you and asked for prayer or you might receive a bit of intuition. If you have no specific targets for prayer, you can simply chant your prayers with the idea that it will be divinely turned into power that can reach whatever person or situation needs that prayer. The act of chanting on prayer beads or *mala* is a practice drawn from Buddhism. The 108 traditional beads each represent a worldly sin, and a practitioner might chant divine names, a personal prayer, or a mantra. Consider chanting, "If it harms none, do what you will." Repeat this 108 times, breathing in with the first half of the phrase, and out with the second. Choose a speed that is comfortable for your breathing. If you relax into this process, it can generate a pleasant trance-like effect. Remember to write down any names of people who come up for you while chanting, as these might be people to add to your prayer list.

Values

So far, I've named values that are important to me that I've learned through my own experiences and from spiritual teachers. Since I know I haven't named every possible value out there, and because you may have some of your own that are different from mine, I'd like you to start thinking about your own deepest values, as they can help guide and inspire your compassionate actions.

Values and the idea of being mindful of harm vary from culture to culture. To enhance our beauty, we often pierce our ears so we can wear earrings. Imagine a culture in which this concept was foreign. First they would see us stabbing holes in our skin. Then, imagine their horror as we intentionally keep the wounds open so we can stick metal and rocks in them. This would seem like incredibly harmful behavior. But of course, we are trading some temporary harm for the greater value, beauty. It is important to know what values you're trading for harm or potential harm. This doesn't mean that you must throw out that value. It just means that you should be conscious about the choices you make, especially if you want to perform actions to mitigate or offset any harm.

Write down a list of your most deeply-held values and think about which ones might be a source of harm. If beauty is a value to you, there may be physical sources of harm such as cosmetic body modifications, plastic surgery, or even manicures and pedicures with a potential for infection. There may be a chance for potential financial harm if spending on beauty products is not carefully budgeted and controlled. There may even be psychological harm if the quest for beauty results in low self-esteem or an eating disorder. You probably mitigate that harm already in many ways. For example, you might only go to licensed, insured, and reputable providers of beauty services. You also probably offset harm by taking care of your body in other ways like eating healthy food and exercising.

If you value adventure and recreation, list some harm that might come from those values. Consider financial harm or harm to the environment as a result of using vehicles for adventure and recreation. Think of any ways you might choose to mitigate or offset that harm. Do this same exercise for each value. Some of the efforts you do to reduce harm may be so instinctual that you forget they exist. However, it's important to be mindful of these things even if the potential for harm is very small.

I didn't care much whether my car had air bags until last week when I was involved in an accident. Now I'm certain that I'll never buy a car without plenty of air bags again. You don't have to experience the worst case scenario or be a worrywart to be mindful about harm reduction. And indeed, I can still choose to ride a motorcycle even though that would place me in potential harm's way, as long as my values are greater than my fears.

Conscious choice and a sense of responsibility are what we're looking for here. Compassion is not as simple as joining up with an ideology or making a single lifestyle choice. You're constantly balancing the potential of harm to others or yourself with your ability to live your life according to your true will and your values, hopefully preserving important relationships in the process. This certainly isn't easy, but perhaps that's why the divine sources that inspired our religions decided to make compassion an important aspect of being mindful. Perhaps the process of thinking your way through all these choices and responsibilities is just as important as preserving the safety and well-being of others and yourself. Look upon this duty as a daily exercise that strengthens your spiritual muscles and builds your spiritual endurance for a life spent well. Even though making these choices is challenging, it shouldn't be viewed with dread or guilt over not being able to attain perfection.

None of us are there yet. When I spoke with a friend of mine who believes in karma, he explained that in his country of origin, nobody achieves enlightenment until everyone achieves it; the community is more important than any individual. I like thinking about karma and the quest to harm none this way, because it's reassuring to know that we're all in this together. It's sort of like when I'm stuck in traffic on the way home and I suddenly realize that everyone around me is also heading home, probably hungry for dinner and missing their families too. It does no good for me to honk the horn and get angry at somebody who cuts me off. We're all getting there at the same speed, and we're all in it together.

Writing Your Own Moral Code and Code of Ethics

Writing out a code of morals and ethics is a useful exercise for several reasons. Firstly, it acts as a means for finding out what you truly believe and for what you stand. This is vital to do before you run into a sticky situation where your morality or ethics are tested. Secondly, your written code can be used like a vision board, attracting moral and ethical behavior into your life. And finally, it's nice to have a reminder that you can post for yourself or even share with others. I have a business code of ethics posted on my website for clients to read. It helps them understand whether or not I share their ethical perspectives on things, and it helps hold me accountable as an ethical business person. I also have a family creed, a statement of some morals and ethics we share. It is posted in several places in our home so when I get stressed out with my family, I can easily see a reminder of our deepest and most cherished values and rein in my behavior. It's the first thing I see when I pull my car into the garage, and the last thing I see when I tuck my kids in at night. I find it helps me calm myself and gain perspective when I'm being tested.

As you can see, this writing exercise may look different depending on your purpose and audience. Instructions appear in this section for several different versions you can create. Write one of them or all of them, if they apply. For all of them you'll need those lists of your most prized virtues, your deepest values, and some of the moral and ethical beliefs that you have already written down in other exercises in this chapter and circled as they pertain to harming none.

Write a Personal Moral Code

Let's start by collecting the information you've already found for yourself. Get out a journal or a piece of paper you can refer to later on. It's a good idea to check back on this personal document once or twice a year to see if some of your beliefs and values have changed with age and experience.

Write down "I value:" and then list some of the circled values that harmonize with compassion. Recall that your deepest values are the things you'd like to spend your time and money on in this lifetime, and remember that you'll have to distill those values down to their purest essence. So while you might value your coin collection, it wouldn't be a deepest value. You might actually be valuing stability as gained through investment or recreation as gained through organizing your coin collection. In this basic form, your values are unlikely to conflict with compassion because there will be a way you can spend your time and money on that value without harming anyone, even if there are other ways that could potentially be dangerous.

Next, write down "I have the following virtues..." Write down the circled virtues you've brainstormed that help you be compassionate. These are traits you already express at least some of the time that might aid you in your quest to live compassionately. It's okay if they sometimes trip you up in your quest; as said before, sometimes our greatest virtues can be our greatest weaknesses. Take for instance the virtue of honesty. Your honesty can help you and others avoid potentially dangerous situations and it reduces harm when you've done something wrong. Though honesty can also result in hurt feelings, it still counts as a virtue that can help you live compassionately.

Write down, "I would like to embody the following virtues:" and list here the virtues that don't yet describe you but that you would like to invite into your life. Patience would be on this list for me. Perhaps by the next time you review this document, you'll be able to switch virtues from this list to the "I have" list.

Finally, write down any morals that can help you live compassionately that might have been left out. You can write them as, "I believe that the following things are inherently good:" and create a list. Sift through the moral codes you may have learned and adapted from spiritual teachers, school, parents, or other sources for anything you may have missed. It's okay to duplicate some of the things that you wrote down as virtues or values. Sometimes there's an awful lot of overlap, and that's a good thing. It means that you have a solid moral system that works well. Write down in your calendar a reminder to review your moral code at the New Year, or perhaps twice a year—once in the spring and once in the fall, when you set your clocks forward and back. When you review your code, you can rewrite it if you have new things to add or rearrange.

Write a Work Code of Ethics

A code of ethics is going to look different from your moral code because it's something that has rules for right behavior. This particular code of ethics is one written for an audience. That audience could be the people with whom you work or the clients or customers you serve. Since your moral code was such a deeply personal document, I wanted to help you write another one that would be more sharable. This code of ethics would be easier to write if you've already written your moral code, so if you haven't done that, you may want to go back and try it. Your moral code informs your code of ethics. Also, your moral code includes lots of key words for virtues and values that you can insert into sentences to make the code of ethics more personalized.

If you work for an organization, you may already have a list of rules, a client bill of rights, or a code of conduct. If any of these documents exist, find and look through them for helpful rules for your behavior that will encourage you to refrain from harm. Write them down first, followed by any rules you'd like to add for your own behavior. Try starting each rule with the sentence "I will ..." and finish up with the rule you've set for yourself to try to follow. Next, offer any assurances of power to clients or coworkers in your working relationship. Try starting sentences with, "You will always ..." For example, "You will always be able to ask me questions and get an honest answer within one business day." Finally, offer assurances of any wrong behaviors you wish to avoid. Try starting a sentence with, "You will never ..." For example, "You will never be asked to share private information."

When you're finished with your code of ethics, check to see if any of your rules overlap or can be combined. You don't want to provide a wall of text and inundate people with information they're never going to read. Once you've got a relatively neat and tidy list, you're ready to hang it on the wall. Make sure to ask the powers that be in your workplace if it's okay to hang your code of ethics somewhere it is visible and readable. Also set a date on your calendar to review it and make sure the code is still viable. It may happen that after you've had it hanging for a while, you'll realize that some of the wording is confusing. It's a good idea to revise regularly if you have time. This can also be used as a good team-building activity with your coworkers, if you have them.

Write a Family Creed

As I wrote before, having a family creed can be very helpful, especially if you have a busy and stressful family life. When writing it, include all the family members who live in your home in this activity. These instructions are geared toward forming the creed with your partner or partners and any children you may have, but it works with any family model. Since you've been reading about ideas like values, virtues, morals, and ethics, you may wish to instruct or at least have a family talk about them. Brainstorm on a big piece of paper first; later you can finalize your family creed and even make it into a nice poster if you like.

To start, write down: "In our family, we value the virtues of …" Here you can mix values and virtues together and brainstorm many terms. Some may overlap, and that's okay. Your family members may pull in some terms from school or work or worship, and that's okay too. Make sure that you all agree on what is written down. If you have children, you may have to help them distill some values down to more abstract concepts, as kids tend to think of concrete examples.

Next, write down some ethics. You can use the subheading "Family Rules" if you have kids, since they may be used to this at school. If it's just a group of adults in your home, you may want to write "Family Agreements" instead so it doesn't have a pushy or condescending connotation. Write down some rules you'd all like to see followed. If there's an opportunity to pull in some vocabulary from your virtues and values, go ahead. For my kids, I made another subheading before some examples. I wrote "Think" and then followed with some of the lines from books and poems that they remembered that exemplify some of the ethical behaviors. It helped them understand but it may be unnecessary if you've got adults in your home or if your children are older. Folks of all ages can add visual aids of drawings or other imagery to inspire you all to join together on this endeavor. Having a family creed can help you feel like you're all on the same side as far as household rules are concerned.

Dealing with Negative People

In traveling your path of compassion, you'll run into people who are downright negative about your attempts. Perhaps you'll find criticism from a parent, boss, or acquaintance who thinks that what you're doing is not good enough or is laughable. You might find somebody who is unsupportive and doesn't care about what you're trying to do. There may be no way to change any of these people's opinions, so you'll have to focus on yourself. Don't let others be the arbiters of justice between you and the universe. It's up to you to decide when you've made things right in your life.

In some religions, harming others is considered a sin or a wrong that ends in some sort of punishment from the divine or a self-imposed penance. Those of us who were raised in households in which naughty behavior was punished may feel like we're getting away with murder whenever we do something harmful, even if we feel bad. Sometimes, the sadness on a loved one's face after I've said something hurtful is worse than a punishment, making me wish I could do some sort of chore to make it all better.

In some religions there are specific prayers that can be said or rituals that can be done as penance or to ask for forgiveness. Until those duties are completed, the penitent is in the doghouse, so to speak. Other religions don't have anything like that, however—there is no "sin" against the divine, or a punishing "hell" to avoid. And of course, if your personal faith has no label, you won't have any accompanying doctrines. Freedom from dogma can be a relief, but it doesn't offer much in the way of reassurance when you're feeling really guilty about something.

A spiritual seeker once came to me and pointed out that some religions don't really have punishments or penance. Even a belief in karma can't really fit the bill as suitable punishment when feeling guilty, since the balance of karma may equalize in many different ways, spread across lifetimes. The seeker told me that in the past, he had done something awful, so awful that he didn't want to talk about it. He wanted my advice on how to spiritually make things right.

I told him first that it was okay to feel bad. The suffering he was experiencing was part of the process of learning his lesson about compassion, a feeling I told him he should own. I asked him to integrate his guilt into the person he is today. Avoiding that guilt is avoiding personal responsibility, a virtue toward which we both are striving. There was no need to ask for forgiveness from any sort of divine being in this case because the divine could not be harmed by his actions. However, I encouraged him to pray simply to talk about his feelings in the same way one might talk openly to a counselor.

He explained to me that there was no way to talk to the person he had wronged or any way to make things right through any kind of direct restitution, which was part of why his guilt was sticking around. If it were possible to apologize and make amends, of course that would have been the best course of action. I told him that another option was to try paying some goodness forward in a way that was related to the problem he caused. For example, if he had injured someone, he could volunteer at a hospital or health care center. If he had damaged property, he could give donations to the poor.

The most important spiritual act one can do in this kind of situation is to make sure the misdeed never happens again. Safeguards could be set up to ensure a similar type of harm would be less likely to happen. Others could be asked to help, objects that caused the harm could be disposed or secured, activities that led to or caused the harm could be discouraged, or those involved could simply take a vow to not let it happen ever again. In this way, the spiritual responsibility is brought back to the seeker try-ing to learn the lesson. Indeed, we are all learning lessons here on earth. We learn by moving forward—we go forth and strive to do the best for all concerned. Included in our moving forward is being gentle with the self and not causing undue self-harm as penance.

three

A Thoughtful Lifestyle: Your Game Plan

In the rosiness of a glass of champagne on New Year's Eve, my resolution to try living a compassionate life seemed like a beautiful thing. But in the harsh light of New Year's Day, reality set in. The goal felt confusingly absolute, and I was loathe to start it that day. It would take an impossible amount of planning to try to change how I lived. Immediately, my mind jumped to all the messages I receive from the world around me about how to minimize harm. I wondered if I'd have to start bicycling everywhere to reduce my carbon footprint. Images flashed in my mind of struggling to lug a trailer full of groceries and my kids uphill in the rain on the side of a dangerous road. Signs from a local animal rights group encouraged me to restrict my diet in a dramatic way, an idea my husband loathed as he is our household cook. Even clapping my hands kills germs, I observed. It was obvious that a practical line would have to be drawn, but the very idea is disillusioning and feels morally messy. Many people give up and walk away, leaving the quandary of compassion for another time. I decided to get my feet wet, and so can you.

How to Do It

How do you envision a compassionate lifestyle you can actually, practically live? It's okay if you believe that people should strive for a life that does absolutely no harm to others, and it's also okay if you take your mindfulness to another focus such as actively helping others. It's also okay to find some middle ground and strive toward more harmless activities in the future while leaving the daily minutiae untouched. The difference is slight, but an absolutist stance means you'll start with a reflective approach, correcting all actions past and present. A proactive, forward-thinking approach is more moderate. Since most people immediately think of the absolutist definition of compassionate living—that is, striving to live as harmless a life as possible—let's create a plan for this lifestyle.

Before you get started, take a moment to acknowledge ideology and put it in its place. Like me, you might easily mix up your own morality with the ideologies of others that have been placed upon you by your culture, the media, or even your friends and family. Here's how to tell the difference.

As discussed in the previous chapter, morality is your own sense of what is good and bad, right and wrong. This itself is largely defined by culture and upbringing, but individuals may vary significantly. My morals tell me that harming others is wrong. Your morals may also dictate to you to what extent harm is okay. For example, when I was a kid I absolutely loved animals. I had a menagerie of pets, dressed as my favorite animal (a bat) for an entire year when I was four years old, and ended up earning a Bachelor of Science degree in zoology. My experiences expanded my sense of compassion to include animals by personal choice. So naturally, I became a vegetarian.

I'm not trying to judge those who do eat meat; the example here is to illustrate that a person's ideas of what constitutes compassion can include very different things, and each of us can feel just as strongly about our morality as personally defined. If I ate a piece of meat, I would feel guilty. My heart rate would increase. I might actually cry and regret it. I'd likely reach out to the divine in prayer to help fortify my resolve or help me avoid future mistakes. An omnivorous person next to me, however, who is just as spiritually strong as myself, might not feel any of these emotions or spiritual crises. The person could also have a mindfulness practice that includes awareness of where their meat comes from, how agricultural reform in our country affects its production and distribution, and as a result, the person could have made vows to eat it sparingly. Either option and many more are okay. The moral absolutes of one person don't necessarily match up to any other. Thus, the battle for compassion is actually an internal one, and specific "sinful" behaviors are not its focus.

Now that you've got a grasp of morality, let's turn to ideology. Ideologies are systems of ideals and ideas that form the basis of sociological, economic, and political theories. That is, ideologies do not exist independently of agendas. You'll need to decide whether you are divorcing yourself from any agenda, or whether you're consciously and purposefully attaching yourself to an ideology you think is objectively superior. To stick to my own vegetarian example, my own personal morals dictate that I would feel sad and guilty if I ate meat because I would feel directly responsible in some way for the death of that animal. If I adopted a vegetarian ideology, I would want to promote vegetarianism to everyone, judge others and feel disgusted when others ate animals, and I would think that the world would generally be a much better place if everyone went vegetarian. That's simply not the case, as I am also compassionate toward others' choices, well aware that omnivores are good people too. Besides, judging others is not the point here!

For another example, let's look at my fears about driving a car. Reducing my environmental footprint is somewhat of a personal moral imperative. If I littered in a beautiful forest or dumped chemicals in the river behind my house, I would feel a visceral reaction of guilt. However, I do not feel this same level of reaction when driving my kids to school. I have been told by others about the effect of oil consumption and car pollution, and I logically know that bicycling everywhere would be the ideal choice for everyone in a utopian world. In this case, my understanding of car use is still at the level of an ideology and has not become a deeply-ingrained moral imperative. Again, others may feel differently, and I have friends who are very committed to lifestyle choices such as bicycling everywhere and only receiving food that has been produced within a hundred miles.

Imagine what it would feel like to suddenly take a vow to completely abstain from harm. What lifestyle choices immediately spring to mind? Chances are, you started thinking of some ideologies but they don't necessarily solve any problems. Witness the inevitable issues with giving money to the homeless or buying newly-marketed electric or hybrid cars that claim to reduce dependence on oils but still use plastics and present new concerns about safe battery disposal.

I believe that the spiritual challenge to live compassionately wasn't meant to be as simple as flipping a switch or as dramatic as making a major lifestyle change. Instead, the desire for compassion should be a constant pull to mindfulness, living in the moment, and connecting with spirit. Having to return to your touchstone wishes for compassion on a daily basis does not represent a failure to live the right way; on the contrary, it shows personal growth.

Balance and Being Practical

Remember that practical barriers are different for everyone, which is why the many religions espousing a compassionate philosophy also ask you to refrain from judging others. Even if your neighbor may seem lackadaisical about her involvement in the community, workplace, her family, or the planet, she may be doing the best she can. And of course when I talk about "harming none," you are included in that directive—don't forget to turn that gentle and nonjudgmental voice on yourself, too. If you're doing the best you can so that it fits your lifestyle right now and you're always striving to improve, you're on the right track.

Striking a balance with practicality is hard. After gauging your immediate reaction to the injunction to harm none and determining what is ideology and what is morality, it's important to address your own deepest morals. Some of them may have already led you down a rabbit hole of what possible actions you can do next in your life. You may have run into barriers that present sticky conundrums of harm to others or simple logistical difficulties. Now is the time to examine them.

For example, everybody knows they're supposed to eat healthy and exercise, no matter what shape the body is in. Neglecting movement and nutrition can cause eventual medical issues in some people. Movement and healthy eating can become a moral imperative for those who believe the body is an expression of spirituality and that compassion includes avoiding self-harm. That said, there are barriers preventing some people from carrying out this moral imperative even to the best of their abilities. Perhaps practical reasons stand in the way, such as a disability or lack of money or access to time and space in which to exercise or find healthy foods. Perhaps your own needs to minimize self-harm run up against the needs to prevent harm to your family. For those in poverty, for example, healthy foods may not go as far on a small budget, and the need to work several jobs and care for children can eliminate opportunities for exercise. The point of this, however, is that someone who has economic barriers should *not* feel guilty or sad.

Getting Over Fear of Hypocrisy

The reason that living a life of compassion or harming none seems like such a lofty goal is that it appears practically impossible; doesn't it make everyone seem like a hypocrite? Watching harm happen to people in your life and community that you can stop can make your goal to harm none seem disingenuous. You may even get flak from cynical friends and family members who point out ways that you've yet to reach your goal. Don't let negativity deter you. In fact, tiny changes can and do make a big difference in the world. Donating small amounts of money, reducing small amounts of waste, turning the purchasing power of just a few products you buy toward fair trade or natural conservation has cumulative good effects. If somebody makes fun of you for not being perfect, don't let it get you down. We all take chances on relationships, career, and spiritual truths. Take the criticism as advice, and see if you can make any more changes.

Nothing we do in life is perfect. It would be foolish to avoid bettering ourselves and the world just because we'll inevitably fall short of perfection. Get past your critical inner gatekeeper. Tell yourself that you're taking baby steps toward making the world and yourself better. You can even set a date ahead in time to do even more. In the beginning, make one small change at a time. And remember that a small change is more likely to stick with you. Tiny tweaks in your lifestyle or the way you think and go about your day can make big changes over time.

Receiving criticism for enthusiastically taking on a compassionate lifestyle is to be expected. When it happens, take a breath and address your own emotional reaction. You may feel automatically defensive, but it would be counter to your goals if you ignored the real harm to yourself or if you fired back with harmful words at the person criticizing you. Take some time out to calm down if you need to. Count to ten, breathe, or even sleep on it before responding if necessary.

Next, allow yourself to open your mind to any truth contained within the criticism, even if the criticism was delivered in a harsh and inappropriate way. Are there any steps you can take to improve yourself along these lines? Are you already in progress on those goals? Don't overwhelm yourself with new and impossible goals. Instead, take a realistic look at why you are choosing to act the way you do.

If necessary, you can then take action to prevent future insults that could shake your resolve. Actions might include spending less time around negative people, or gently asking the person to talk with you in a different way. Tell him or her how the comment made you feel, and give some concrete advice about what you need in the future from him or her to avoid those hurt feelings.

Exploration

Trying to live a compassionate lifestyle requires an adventurous spirit. You'll need to explore your world in new ways including digging for knowledge about how you might be causing others harm. Facing these truths will feel uncomfortable. Ignorance is bliss, as they say. If you find out that your favorite t-shirt company has harmful employment practices, your best makeup is tested on animals, the fast food company on your way home from work funds atrocious political goals, or your go-to brand of sugar is processed with bone char, it will be disheartening, depending on your own personal path. Becoming more mindful of potential sources of harm in the world might seem to increase the world's lousy nature exponentially. But you know that's not true—all the problems you uncover in your world were still there before you knew about them. Your knowledge empowers you to make a change, even if it is a small one.

It's okay to experiment and even fail at making lifestyle choices designed to lessen your harmful effect on the world. Experimentation with different ways of doing things can be fun. Don't let yourself fall into the all-or-nothing trap of doing everything perfectly. Slip-ups are okay. It takes a while to establish a routine, so don't beat yourself up. For example, if I want to reduce my self-harm by eating healthier, it can be easy to obsess over virtuous or right eating. This is not healthy and can be downright pathological.

Don't get lost in a forest of details when finding your new path to compassion. Be kind and forgiving to yourself as a way to continuously reduce harm. Don't try to make a dozen lifestyle changes at once, unless you really live a relaxed life and have lots of resources to help you out, such as a supportive family, workplace, and plenty of free time to think over your choices. Instead, try implementing one thing at a time. Once you've established one new habit and are successful on a fairly regular basis, you can move on to another change.

It can be overwhelming to overhaul your life, even one thing at a time. Try giving yourself short homework assignments. Then put them on your calendar so you'll get things done. For example, one day I decided I would only use cosmetics that were not tested on animals. I set aside an hour one day to go through all of my bathroom drawers, find the cosmetics, look them up online, and if necessary, call the companies to find out if they fit my new directive to cause less harm. That day I was able to find out which cosmetics to put on my shopping list and which ones to replace with less harmful products. If I had never set aside that time, the chore simply wouldn't have been done.

In another effort to reduce harm to our planet, my husband took charge of switching our household to using cloth bags for groceries instead of disposable plastic bags. For this simple system to work, he had to make sure that we had enough cloth bags to hold all our groceries, and that they were all in his vehicle on time for grocery day. After unloading groceries, the cloth bags would then have to be immediately placed back into the vehicle for the next shopping trip. It sounds pretty straightforward, but if a new routine is not made into a habit, it won't happen. Don't be ashamed of setting alarms or notifications to remind yourself to do things while you're learning a new habit.

Part of exploration is research. It's good to find out which actions might cause harm to the earth, to people on the other side of the world, or to your community. However, don't forget that some of the research can be done with those you meet face to face. There may be ways you communicate with others or perceive them that affect your close relationships. Don't get overwhelmed with research into compassionate alternatives to everyday activities. Remember, anything can be broken down into smaller steps or increments of time. Compassionate living is not easy, but each habit can become easier when it becomes part of your routine.

Unintentional Harm

Our first understandings of how we harm others comes to us sometime in the toddler and preschooler years. I can recall one instance in which my three-year-old daughter had a rip-roaring tantrum that involved a lot of screaming and kicking the floor. As I carried her to her bedroom for a time-out, she pummeled me wildly with her tiny fists, her body contorting out of control with rage. Big feelings were coming out of a tiny body, taking the form of hitting and kicking.

As she took deep breaths and lay in her bed to calm down, I had to check in with my own emotions as well. My feelings were hurt because one of the people I loved most in the world had just punched and kicked me in anger. When we were both feeling emotionally ready to talk about it, she was still a little angry and told me with teary eyes that she didn't want to apologize. I asked her if she wanted to hurt me, and she answered with an emphatic "No!" She was shocked that I could suggest such a thing. I explained to her that hitting hurts, and it made her pause for a moment. It evidently had never occurred to her that hitting a big person such as myself could actually hurt the person. Then she apologized and gave me a hug.

As adults, most of the harm we do is likely to be unintentional. Unless you're struggling with your career path or a life situation that you know generates a great degree of harm, the little unintentional things are what are probably the most disturbing to you. When told that something you did caused harm, you might immediately react with denial or embarrassment. It can seem like the accusation is actually telling you that you're careless, rude, or downright foolish. Like my child (or myself in my immature moments), you might say some things to try to minimize the situation or defend your actions.

Dismissing unintentional harm is a natural reaction, and it is worth giving it some thought. Great philosophers such as Immanuel Kant proposed that the intentions rather than the outcome of actions are what count toward being a morally good person. That's all well and good, but in the real world we know that hurting somebody even unintentionally doesn't make us feel like good people. We should follow these feelings and try to do the right thing in the future. Here are some steps you can take if you unintentionally harm someone.

First, let the person vent to you without interruption. Sometimes, a lot of the harm can be negated just by letting the other person share his or her feelings. You may feel the desire to defend yourself, especially if the claims about harm are exaggerated. Try simply listening instead. Next, allow yourself to honestly deliver any apologies that need to be given. You might say, "I'm sorry for..." and explain the action you did and why it was wrong. Then, explain how in the future you will not do the same harmful act or a similar harmful act. Try patching up the relationship by asking explicitly and openly for forgiveness. You can't force another person to forgive you, of course, but you can certainly open the door.

After validating the other person's feelings, it's appropriate to offer solutions to the problem. Perhaps listening and offering an apology was all that was needed. Or the two of you might be able to brainstorm a way that will make the situation right. If not, the only solution may be sincerely vowing to not repeat the act of harm in the future.

Don't beat yourself up too much about unintentional harm. Know that all you can do is try to improve yourself in the future. It's not necessarily a poor reflection on your personality if you unintentionally harm people, as it might be just bad luck or simply because you put yourself out there interacting with others. If you start to notice a pattern of unintentional harm, you may be able to do some active self-improvement.

For example, if you're constantly angering roommates or fellow drivers on the road, you might naturally be a bit absentminded and oblivious as to how your actions affect others. This is a problem you can work on and implement appropriate changes to. If you're shifting your focus to others, eliminating your insensitivity is the single most important component of being more mindful. If you notice that you consistently make sarcastic jokes that hurt others, it might be a pattern. You'll need to take note and break that habit.

Above all, unintentional harm can be combatted with mindfulness. Becoming mindful of others requires a sense of empathy and a conscious check-in with how others around you are affected by your words and actions. If you're a naturally empathetic person, unintentional harm may make you feel incredibly guilty. If this is the case, allow yourself to let go after you've done all you can to make a situation right. If you're not a naturally empathetic person, you may need to force yourself to imagine the world from somebody else's point of view. This thought exercise may seem fakey at first, but over time it can become a natural mindfulness step you can take, and it can be as quick as taking a deep breath before speaking.

Offsetting Harm

An eighty-year-old Holocaust survivor named Dr. Alex Hershaft decided to make a difference and reduce harm in the world by becoming an activist for animal rights. Why did he do this? He found a parallel in the human suffering he witnessed during the war and the suffering he saw in factory farmed animals. "Never again" is the phrase used by the Jewish community to memorialize the atrocities they endured. So even though he had no particular affinity for animals prior to learning about their pain, he now took up the cause for animal rights. He organized a "Fast Against Slaughter" spiritual fasting and awareness event held annually in October. This man had seen a terrible harm in the world that had resulted in the deaths of millions of his people. Nothing could undo that tragedy, so he chose to champion another cause that was important to him. He made a direct connection between his own experience of harm and something he felt he could do to better the world. Of course, he could have chosen other things as well but this particular connection made sense in his own mind. When you choose to offset harm, you can also make connections or simply work to try to make the world a better place.

For example, some people purchase carbon offsets in order to reduce their environmental footprint on the planet. Sometimes these offsets can be purchased directly from your electric company; they typically help pay for windmills and solar panels to generate electricity. Several independent companies such as TerraPass also sell offsets that fund alternative energy. Carbon dioxide and monoxide are released when we drive cars and fly airplanes. There are companies that sell carbon offsets, which are basically tickets that count for the same amount of trees to be planted or wind energy to be generated or other offset activity to "make up" for the carbon-related harm visited on the planet. Realistically, this doesn't make the harm not happen, but it is one way of mitigating harm that satisfies people because the offset is connected directly to the harm being done. In this example, a person would be purchasing an offset just for him- or herself or a single family, not trying to make up for everyone else on the planet.

Another example of offsetting harm is by choosing an injustice in the world and trying to make it better no matter what your connection is to that injustice, if any. For example, if you have a heart for the issue of domestic violence, you could volunteer in a shelter and collect supplies for the residents there to use. Some people do this kind of volunteering and involvement because of personal experience with domestic violence, but others do it simply to make the world better. What you choose to do doesn't have to necessarily tie in with any harm you've personally experienced in the past, either as aggressor or victim. After all, it's not meant to be a punishment that fits a crime. Offsetting harm means you're putting spiritual energy into the betterment of the world, hopefully in equal or greater measure than harm.

Offsetting harm is a complicated subject. Some people worry about divine retribution, with a fatherlike God visiting punishment down upon them. In chapter 4 we'll explore some more beliefs and attitudes regarding divine balance. For now, think of being a kindly parent to yourself. If a toddler broke a vase in your house, you might encourage her to make things right by trying to fix the vase or saving up for a new one. If neither option will replace the value of the vase, you know that she can make it up to you in other ways to restore your happiness over time. Though permanent in the life span of that vase, the harm is not permanent in your relationship. In fact, relationships are give-and-take things that encompasses many cycles of harm and making things right. Use this analogy with yourself and the harm you visit on the world.

You don't have to beat yourself up about the small stuff in the long term. Each time you work hard to make amends or offset harm, you're exercising your mind and spirit. You're building something in the world and learning something about yourself at the same time. This cycle of learning may be one reason for our spiritual journey on this earth.

Do No Harm But Take No Bull

Being relatively harmless doesn't mean becoming a doormat. Since we're talking about progressive reduction of harm, you know eventually you'll need to deal some harm both unintentionally and purposefully. Some harm will be tough love, like the incision a surgeon makes to heal an injury or a disease.

Some harm might be in self-defense, a special case or exception for many people. Opinions differ on the spiritual consequences for causing harm in self-defense. Some especially peaceful paths encourage never lashing out. Even when confronted with violence, this perspective asks you to take up no defense and to trust in divine justice. When met with passivity, an aggressor may indeed back down.

Other spiritual paths encourage one to be peaceful and loving with friends, kin, and neighbors, but allow exceptions when dealing with dangerous foes. These warrior paths stress that discernment is key. There are still legal, physical, emotional, and spiritual consequences for causing harm, even in self-defense. Causing serious injury to another even when defending yourself is not a decision to be made lightly. However, protecting the self or loved ones can sometimes be worth whatever universal consequences are likely to be dealt to all parties concerned. This gamble is a deeply personal decision, so it's not something I like to judge others or even myself for, as many of us have points in life when we felt particularly vulnerable. Just as declawed cats can bite out of fear and be more dangerous than cats with claws, vulnerable people can be loose cannons.

For reasons of mindful self-defense, many take up training in martial arts. I did it myself, winning some competitions and forging lifelong friendships in the process. I learned quite a lot about self-defense and many more things about peace from my friend, Sensei Wheeldon, who sadly has died of pancreatic cancer. Sensei Wheeldon was an amazing person. Even though he was nearly blind, he was a skilled karate master, working his way up through the black belt ranks all the way up to the month of his death. He taught me that it is not only your physical senses that are used when you sense danger. He didn't need to rely on his aged and faulty eyes when skillfully blocking attacks. These classes weren't just shadow boxing; sparring could generally guarantee a few nasty bruises, a racing pulse, a limp now and again, and a triumphant smile when lucky.

Sensei Wheeldon taught me how to sense the energy emanating from somebody intending to do harm. It rolls across the room like thick waves. He taught me that there are indeed times when a good offense, replete with fearsome displays of power, are key to getting an adversary to step down. He also taught me how to defend myself with a mind to gain the upper hand and end a conflict as quickly as possible. I will never forget Sensei Wheeldon, as he was one of the greatest teachers of my life. Before I joined his karate class, I felt a lot of frustration and would often lash out at others verbally, mimicking the physical tantrums I had as a small child. Through training, I recognized my inner power and as a result felt less ready to lash out in self-defense against minor threats. Training in martial arts or even archery or other target shooting can lead one to be less likely to inflict harm.

It is my belief that those who seek to live compassionately do not have to be vulnerable victims or doormats. We can strive for peacefulness with loved ones and the important relationships in life while still standing strong against potential wrongdoers. There is a trade-off, of course. And the better prepared you are to defend yourself, the more quickly and accurately you will make decisions when the time comes. It's best to decide your own stance on peacefulness or self-defense before the universe presents you with an opportunity to live your values. Consider strongly, now, what you would do if someone threatened you with harm. Would it make a difference to you if this person was a stranger? A loved one? An estranged family member? Would you be able to live with yourself if you caused somebody extreme harm, even if it was in self-defense?

Aside from situations in which one might need to use deadly force, the more frequent application of this philosophy is with minor emotional episodes. Remember how a person intending harm can have energy rolling off of them in waves? Well, the more sensitive people among us can feel very negatively affected by that energy. You'll know you're one of these sensitive people if you can sense fear, anger, and generally disorganized and chaotic intentions in those around you. If you've ever been in a crowd or had a negative person enter the room and felt dizzy, sick, exhausted, or agitated, these could be energetic effects.

When experiencing these negative sensations, the natural reaction might be to snap or otherwise spread that negativity. Instead, you can perform some simple energy-working exercises as acts of compassion that defend yourself at the same time. These energy exercises are called "grounding," because the idea is to send that negative energy harmlessly into the earth where it can be renewed as positive energy and used for different things. There are many ways to ground, and in a little bit I'll cover a special grounding procedure designed with the axiom "harm none" in mind. I use the technique when I find myself overpowered with negative emotions when interacting with other people. Sometimes a situation is obvious, such as when someone directly insults or acts irresponsibly toward you. But there are other kinds of people who can cause those negative feelings or have that chaotic kind of energy about them.

Energy Vampires

They sound like weird creatures from horror films, but energy vampires (sometimes "psychic vampires") are types of people, not mythological creatures at all! These kinds of people thrive on others' energy so much that their very presence feels draining. Anyone who has worked or volunteered serving the general public will recognize the feeling of a specific person's interactions causing mental and physical exhaustion. If there's an energy vampire in your life, you'll dread this person's phone calls or visits, and dealing with them can leave you feeling like you've run a marathon, even if the person isn't saying or doing anything particularly provocative. I once had a friend who was an energy vampire. After interacting with her, I'd have to give myself a time-out for the rest of the day just to rest and recuperate my energy.

There are several ways of dealing with energy vampires. Grounding is one way, and you'll find a grounding exercise below this one. Grounding your own energy when an energy vampire is around is like plugging yourself into a wall outlet instead of letting the vampire drain your energy completely. It can mitigate the harmful effects of having your life energy stolen from you. Another option is creating your own energetic shield, a technique for which is found in a later exercise. Shields can prevent the energy vampire from taking your energy at all.

In the long run, the best option for dealing with energy vampires is to eliminate them from your life if at all possible. The reason for this is because you have to concentrate and focus every time you ground or shield to deal with the problem, and this solution is not practical for the long term. The mental tax of constantly being on guard can be almost as bad as "feeding" the energy vampire him- or herself.

Cutting off an energy vampire may not seem like the compassionate thing to do but it is. Firstly, the energy vampire doesn't need to feed off others. It is a habit the energy vampire has either learned to rely on or chosen. If you set healthy boundaries with the person, he or she may experience the consequences of losing you as a wake-up call to learn more appropriate behaviors. Or they may figure out what's up and move on to the next victim.

To eliminate energy vampires from your life, first identify those vampires and decide whether it is possible and practical to cut them out of your life. The most compassionate thing to do may be to tell the person why you are setting the boundaries you are if the energy vampire has been a close friend or family member. Think of cutting off your energy vampire as a break-up. Ideally, you will set a date with them in a public place and use an I-based message to tell the person what you need. For example: "When you come by my house unannounced after work, I feel agitated and exhausted. I need you to keep our interactions limited to the workplace from now on." If the energy vampire is just an acquaintance, there's no need to make a big show of letting that person go; it may be enough to simply delete that person's contact information so you won't be tempted to contact him or her again.

Grounding

Step 1) Give yourself a time-out. Doing so allows you the time and space to gain control over your body and mind. I like to take a knee wherever I am; that is, stoop down onto one knee and bow my head. This stops me from any tantrum-like behaviors such as slamming doors, tossing something, or generally moving my body in an agitated way. Another option is to leave the space in which you're experiencing negative energy.

Step 2) Connect with the earth. Close your eyes and feel your connection to the earth beneath your feet. Even if you're in a tall building or on a bus, imagine that you have roots or a conduit that can snake down to the earth below. As I write these words, I'm on an airplane, but I can visualize tendrils of light that anchor me to my Mother Earth even as I am in transit. Feel the energy of the earth. Some people feel it as a warmth, chill, tingling, buzzing, humming, fuzziness, or gentle pressure.

Step 3) Ground negative energy harmlessly into the earth. Take deep breaths and know that the energy is being harmlessly taken by the earth for renewal and transformation. Discharge any anger, fear, or other negative emotions and energy through your feet into the earth. You can touch the earth with your hands if you choose. Try to feel the energy as it leaves your body and push it with your mind. You can even visualize the energy in your mind's eye, if it will help. Some people see negative energy as a vibrant light, smoke, or swirling darkness. When this stage of the process is complete, you should feel your blood pressure lower, your heart rate slow, and your muscles begin to relax.

Step 4) Draw gentle, positive energy harmlessly from the earth. Allow the peaceful earth energy to refuel and rejuvenate you. Some people visualize this energy as a bright light or refreshing water. Try to feel this energy. When this stage of the process is complete, you should feel alert and relaxed but calm.

This grounding technique can be used whenever you feel overwhelmed and have the potential to harm someone with your words, mannerisms, tone of voice, or actions in a situation. This grounding time-out should allow you time to reset yourself before speaking and resolving the situation. The resolution, of course, may be to walk away. You can also ground yourself in preparation for an interaction or a place that you know is going to be stressful and put you on a defensive edge.

Another energetic technique you can use as a preventative measure is shielding. In this sense, shielding is protecting yourself with an energy bubble so that negative energy from a person, place, or situation cannot affect you. It can be used in conjunction with grounding when you know that your patience and tolerance is going to be tested. For example, shielding is great if you're going to be in a noisy and crowded place or if you are going to confront somebody about a topic of conflict. The following shielding exercise is adapted from one originally designed by author and activist Starhawk, and it is especially suited to the goals of compassion.

Shielding Exercise

Imagine you are surrounded by bubbles of energy in the colors of the rainbow. The first layer, closest to your skin, is red, then surrounding that aura is a layer of orange, then, yellow, green, blue, purple, indigo, and finally violet. Notice that you can make the colors as vibrant or as muted as you like. Observe that you can also make the layers as thick or as thin as you choose.

As harmful energies come to you, visualize them any way you like. They can be dark and smoky swirls of energy, house-flies, or even dodge balls. As they try to pass through to you, imagine they get stopped at one of the rainbow layers. Perhaps some bounce right off the outermost violet shield, while harmful ones dissipate as soon as they get close enough to hit your red layer.

Likewise, imagine your harmful thoughts and feelings are stopped by these layers as well. In order for a good thought or feeling to get out to the outside world, it has to pass safely through each and every layer of that rainbow shield. Only the most true and worthy of them will succeed.

When I was a schoolteacher for teenagers, I found grounding and shielding exercises to be a vital daily practice. Every teacher needs to at least be naturally skilled in subconsciously shielding and grounding to survive the job. Every day, some adolescents will throw death-dagger glares in the direction of a teacher, fling hateful insults, and basically distill every last drop of hormone-addled angst into a weapon against the injustice of authority figures. I was working at an alternative school, so for some of the students it was the end of the road and a last chance at education after repeated problems with authority. I loved all my students. There's something special about a teen who is certain of him- or herself and who advocates at all costs for even the slightest perceived injustice. It's endearing, really.

For kids, love is not enough, however. It is my humble opinion that a lack of grounding and shielding against the very real effects of harmful energies from others is one reason for the high turnover rate among teachers. The phenomenon can be observed in other industries too, such as when counseling people who have experienced abuse and hardship. It's tough dealing head-on with all of those feelings and energies from past harms. That's where your shield is necessary. You can't just process it all. If you want to abstain from harm, chances are you're working with people to rectify past hurts, but you can't be the lightning rod for the world. You'll have to allow some things to bounce off of you so you can take care of yourself.

The Proactive Interpretation of Compassion

As mentioned earlier, some interpret the spiritual injunction to be compassionate as encouragement to seek out harmless activities rather than to try to modify all life to fit some completely safe, harm-free mold. This encouragement is expressed well in the saying, "If it harms none, do what you will." The logic is clear: the order is not to refrain from harming anyone but to do what you truly will. If it is your deepest heart's desire to do it, you must. Follow your bliss. Don't let anything turn you aside, especially not complacency or apathy. In this case, compassion is an invitation to be passionate. If it doesn't hurt anyone and it makes you happy, get out there and do it!

This may be a confusing way to look at the topic of compassion for some. It may seem odd to relinquish the constant worry about preventing harm. Instead, the proactive view asks you to turn that enthusiastic brain power to the topic of what you want to spend your time doing that is harmless. If you fill up all of your time and space with these activities, you'll end up with no room left over in life to plot any kind of harm.

Compassion: The Proactive View

Implementing an "if it harms none, do what you will" proactive lifestyle requires a different manner of thinking. Instead of thinking about your past and present, you'll turn to your future plans. This can feel motivating, but you might also feel a little guilty during the process. Since you're reading this, you're probably a naturally very responsible person. The idea of acknowledging that you probably perform little acts of harm on a daily basis may feel irksome. If you find yourself feeling like a hypocrite, just remember that the more you fill your future life with activities free from harm, the more you will eliminate less savory interactions from your life.

For a fun way to get started, I encourage you to brainstorm a list of things you feel inspired to do in life. Perhaps there's a dusty musical instrument sitting in your closet that you want to pick up and play. Perhaps you've been procrastinating on buying a gym membership. Maybe you have the next great novel bouncing around in your head. Or perhaps you've even been thinking about switching careers or going back to school.

Next to each item on your list, write down some of the immediate harm that might come from each action. This might feel more familiar: you've probably already gone over the pros and cons in your head for each of these actions. Think about the harm that might come to yourself as well as the harm that might come to others. Allow yourself to make connections to future harm that might come about as a result of or reaction to the actions you do. It may seem counterproductive to think about worst-case scenarios, but remember the point is to find harmless actions, not rule out everything in your life that can cause harm.

When you're finished, see if any items on your list have no harmful outcomes. There might be conditions for some of your activities to make them harmless. For example, if you want to write a novel, you may have to do so only during times when you're not working or caring for family. This is okay. If some items on your list don't result in harm, go for it and make plans to do them. Even if the goal is a large one, you can take a small step toward that goal today. For example, you could look up further information about that goal.

If there aren't any items on your list that don't cause some level of harm, that's good news as well. It means you're a very conscientious person and have thought about the many potential avenues for harm. But any potential doesn't mean you shouldn't do any of these actions on your list, at least if you're using the proactive interpretation of compassion. For the purposes of this exercise, I encourage you to brainstorm more things for your list, perhaps thinking of smaller and more manageable goals for the day or week ahead.

If this exercise works for you, keep on doing it. Try a weekly meditation in which you plan new things for your life. At some point, you'll reach a sort of equilibrium in which your life is full of amazing things, but you can't quite fit in any more without causing harmful decline to your work or family life. This is a perfect place to be, because then you can take time to list things more sparingly. It might work to save it as a monthly task or even as a New Year's resolution activity.

Creating a Game Plan

Now that you've seen the two approaches to compassion (the reflective and the proactive), you can begin to plan how to implement these in your own life. You may notice that the two interpretations dovetail to form a more all-inclusive game plan for your entire life. It may seem overwhelming, but you can use both of these approaches over and over again, leapfrogging to make improvements in your effect on the world.

Here's the general game plan as it might work in your life: Start proactively. Brainstorm a list of activities, and choose one that is harmless. If you can't think of any, push yourself to find something small and simple. For example: painting a picture, starting a new volunteer job, learning to play the ukulele, walking the dog twice a day instead of once, or calling your mom just to chat once a week. Starting small will train your brain to think in a positive way, and it will motivate you to do some good and have some fun. Don't overwhelm yourself with too many life changes all at once. You can try one small new thing a day or develop a grander plan with a goal months away.

Once you've had some success with the proactive approach, it's time to look at your present life and do some pruning. Again, start with a positive attitude. Make a list of your deepest values in life. This is a good bridging activity between being proactive about compassionate goals and being reflective about harming none in daily life. For example, you might value health, family, the environment, or social equality. You may have a heart for helping a specific group of people, like the mentally ill, battered women, or children suffering from cancer. Reexamine any values that don't seem to make sense. For example, if you wrote down that you value money, do you actually value stability or freedom? If you wrote down that you value travel, you might actually value adventure or recreation.

Looking back on your list of values, you may find that this activity helps hone and focus your proactive list of compassionate activities. You can brainstorm from each value some things you might wish to do that are related to increasing the quality of time with that value in your life. If adventure is one of your values, you might wish add more activities on your list that have to do with travel, exploration, or learning exciting and new sports and skills. Maybe you'll plan a road trip with some good friends or rent a cabin and go camping with family. Your list of values is also an important thing to keep on hand when you're deciding how your lifestyle can become more harm-free.

There may be some actions you do that can be tweaked in small ways to improve the world according to your values. If you're an environmentalist who's passionate about recycling, chances are you'd never drop an aluminum can in a garbage can in public. You might walk down an extra hallway to get to the recycling bin. But in your own home, you might throw away boxes and other small paper items in the bathroom wastebasket rather than walking all the way to a recycling bin in the kitchen. A simple action would be for you to vow to walk the extra few feet, or to place an extra recycling bin in the bathroom for easy access. These simple adjustments to your life won't be earth-shattering changes, but over time they can cumulatively make a difference.

For some people, changing many habits will be relatively easy, but for others it is difficult. It helps if you have more resources for coping, such as supportive friends and family, an income that can facilitate lifestyle changes, and free time. If you have none of these things or you have other barriers, don't beat yourself up about the changes you cannot make. Some of the gentlest people I know in life are also the most impoverished and have the least resources. It would break my heart to think that they feel lesser than somebody who is able to afford the most sustainably harvested and ethically traded this or that. Look instead for doors that are open to change in your life, and make one small change at a time.

A major life change is needed for some people who want to align their actions with their inner values. If this isn't the case for you, don't worry; it's not something you have to search for or scratch your head over. The sort of ethical quandaries I'm talking about are "elephant in the room" situations such as being passionate about eradicating lung cancer from the earth but working for a cigarette company. Maybe you feel trapped in a toxic marriage that is harming both parties. There are probably downsides to making change in situations like these, and some of those downsides might even look harmful. Quitting an unethical job can cause a financial crisis. Asking for a divorce can cause emotional panic or an unstable living situation.

In situations that present moral contradictions, you'll have to bring out your fairness scales and make a judgment. List those pros and cons with an eye toward true harm. For example, the harm caused by a loveless marriage may outweigh the idea of being compassionate toward a spouse that wants to stay together. Note that some harm is inevitable and transient. When doctors take the Hippocratic oath to "first do no harm," it means they're still allowed to make surgical cuts that bleed, hurt, and could cause serious complications, because the benefit of the treatment outweighs the harm. In the end, there is most likely no lasting harm, or at least it is the physician's intent to not inflict it. So put on your surgeon's thinking cap and think about any areas of your life you already know require major surgery, because right now they're on life support.

Reflection and Evaluation: All in Good Time

Making changes is tough. If you're the sort of person who has quit exercise plans, housecleaning goals, or beauty regimens before, you'll know what I mean. If you can't do everything perfectly in the first few days or weeks of a new lifestyle plan, it may seem like it's time to give up. But give yourself time to adjust to new goals. If your life changes never have a fair chance to succeed, you'll always switch from one new thing to another. Building in regular checkpoints to reflect on your progress is vital for success.

As you progress toward your goals, make sure that you choose a point in time to stop and evaluate. You can pursue even the most idealistic of goals if you have an end point in mind. For example, if you wanted to try a radical new diet that only uses foods sourced within a hundred miles of your home because you're passionate about sustainable food production practices, you can set a goal of trying the diet for a week or a month. Setting a limit before you even get started may sound like cheating or like you're not serious about your goal. But this limit will keep you from quitting three days into your attempt when your grocery list starts looking boring and unappealing, or when you realize that you might have to seek out a local farmer's market before getting a vital ingredient for your favorite dessert.

At the end of your specified point in time, you might have a pretty good idea about whether it's working for you or not. If everything is going swimmingly, you can extend the amount of time to stick to your new lifestyle change by weeks, months, or a year. You can also add on a new and different lifestyle change and shift your focus. If things are going horribly wrong, it is safe to abandon that change and try a new one instead. You might want to focus on something entirely different so you won't get too disheartened about the process. For example, if you're passionate about sustainable food practices and the restriction to a hundred-mile radius was a bust, you can make a plan to start a garden or to recycle more of your food packaging, or to focus on one product in your diet at a time.

If you find that your attempt falls somewhere between success and failure, that's okay too. It may be that you simply need to extend the time that you are working on your goal because your initial estimate was a little too optimistic. It's good to take a breath and look at the situation. You might want to turn to other resources to make your goal a little more feasible. Here are some questions you can ask yourself while reflecting on your progress.

What is Going Well About My Attempts to Be More Compassionate?

Look first for the positives in your new life path. Even if you've lessened harm or cheered someone up just a little bit, celebrate that change. If you have measurable results such as "I yelled at my sister only once this week instead of at dinner every night," you can write those things down. It can be empowering to review your attempts week after week and see the gradual changes for the better. Otherwise, you might become focused on every small failure.

What Could Be Done Better?

Now take account of all the obvious slip-ups. There may have been unintentional harm as well as cheating on your goals. Think about why the mistake occurred, and take note of any patterns that give you clues about the problem. For example, if you said rude things to your husband that weren't very compassionate, you might notice that you snap more at others when you stay up late and are tired. Or perhaps you were feeling hungry and cranky when you were a bit short with a coworker. Be realistic if your slip-ups were entirely unpreventable. Don't feel entirely responsible if it can't be helped. Decide whether the failures were just flukes or they're indicative that your plan is not sustainable. For example, imagine you care about the impact fossil fuels have on the environment and are trying to take your bicycle instead of your car for transport. If you used your car more than you expected, it could have been a fluke due to picking someone up at the airport, or it could be because cold weather, long distances, and kids in car seats make that plan impractical for you at this stage of your life. The only way you'll know for sure is if you record some data about your attempts to make changes in your life. Keep a log or a journal if you're unsure.

What Will I Do Next?

Decide on a game plan for your next goal. Choose between extending the time frame and seeing how things go, or scaling back on your current goal, or starting a new goal. For example, if you were trying to start a new side business selling knitted scarves for charity and you only made one sale in the month, you have a choice to make. If you're hoping this business will be so successful that you can fund the opening of a new homeless shelter, obviously that isn't working yet. Either try another month to see whether sales increase, scale back your hopes to fund the shelter and settle for paying for some food for the homeless, or try starting a different business selling candles or something else. Make sure not to overwhelm yourself with too many changes at once. If you're still faltering at starting your new habit, even if things are going well, go ahead and give yourself more time to settle into a routine. If however you feel like your successful changes are already part of your life for good, you can choose a new goal. It can be related or entirely new. Remember to carefully go through the possible and probable harms associated with new life activities before undertaking them, and make provisions if needed to prevent any harm.

The Importance of Progress

It's important to track your progress and to keep moving forward with your goals. Every religious tradition teaches that compassion is a practice of mindfulness rather than an end-state everyone can achieve. Becoming complacent can be the enemy of this mindfulness, even if you have positive intent. It's easy to become sanctimonious and think, "I just donated blood, so I don't have to worry about how I'm affecting others today," or "I'm vegan, so I'm already as harmless as can be." Some of the most frequent causes of harm are relational harm stemming from hurtful words and actions, and those will never be completely eliminated from life. One must stand constant loving guard at one's thoughts. You aren't being punished for being human; this isn't a chore. Think of this process as a way to dig deep into the true nature of harm in the universe and to become closer to the divine source of peace and gentleness.

Ultimately, the careful accounting you're doing draws your focus to others and keeps it there. Harm reduction is one step along the path of compassion. In a study conducted on nurses to try to reduce harm caused by things like patients falling down in the ward, researchers made an interesting discovery. They noticed that when the nurses focused on seeing people as people instead of simply focusing on reducing harm, they actually were more successful at preventing falls. After compassion training and focusing on the humanity of their patients, falls went down from three falls in three months to zero falls in three months (Day, 974–978). Let go of all the worry and simply see people as people.

The Nature of Harm

I'd like you to ponder the true nature of harm. Though all religious traditions encourage people to avoid harming others unduly, the idea of harm is very subjective. If you only do to others what you would like done to you, the assumption is that you have an average understanding and experience of suffering and that the other person you are considering does also. However, you may have a very high or low threshold for suffering due to experiences and ability. The others you deal with on a daily basis may likewise have very different thresholds for suffering, which may be why "harm none" is actually a simplified version of the idea of mitigating or lessening harm.

Consider what harm means to you at its essential level. Try thinking about self-harm in addition to harm inflicted on others. Do you have equally strong feelings about both? Some spiritual traditions put the other before the self so harm to others is seen as more egregious than harm to the self, yet self-harm is also frowned upon as a sign of carelessness or a manifestation of mental illness. Often times we must listen carefully to others to determine harm. I tend to be a person who likes to make jokes, so a frequent source of unintentional harm is when I make a joke that would not bother me but seriously irks a friend or family member. For example, I am often teased about my love for country music. When I lovingly teased my husband for his own choice in music during a time when he felt stressed out, he took it pretty hard. Even though it doesn't harm me when people make fun of my taste in music, it can still harm others when I make fun of theirs. The art of listening and being attentive to signs of harm is one that needs cultivation for living a compassionate lifestyle.

In search of obvious signs of harm, we may miss the more subtle forms that pervade daily existence in more privileged settings. The sort of harm that first springs to mind is bodily harm; harm that can cause illness, injury, or death. Let's extend that definition: for a thought exercise, consider harm to body, mind, and spirit.

Emotional abuse is defined by its ability to cause psychological trauma such as anxiety, depression, and post-traumatic stress disorder. Most mental harm of this nature happens in abusive relationships, but more mild forms of mental harm can be caused in everyday situations. Most commonly this is talked about in the public sphere as shaming, bullying, or insensitivity. Being mindful about mental harm doesn't mean you have to try to make the world all nice all the time; however, if it is a goal of yours to reduce mental harm, it may do some good to monitor your own thoughts and phrase things in a tactful way.

Spiritual harm has a more amorphous definition. Certainly some cults promote spiritual abuse. Also, preventing somebody from following his or her religion freely may cause spiritual harm. Spiritual harm can also become a catch-all for harm that is so pervasive that it defies categorization. An example of this is systemic racism. To combat these all-encompassing forms of harm, many people turn to the divine as a source of peace and love. However, spreading the "harm none" mindset in the outer world may be another practical way to make a difference. More information on that can be found in the final chapter.

four

Steps Along the Path to a Peaceful Existence

In 1953, an ordinary woman changed her life one day after an extended period spent in meditation and prayer. This simple woman was raised on a farm, and she turned to peace activism later in life. She had an unforgettable smile and beautiful wisps of snow-white hair, but on that day she gave up her name. She donned simple garments colored blue to symbolize compassion. On her shirt, the words "Peace Pilgrim" were printed in white, as this was the name she chose to take on. For the remaining twenty-eight years of her life, she walked across the United States unceasingly while spreading a non-denominational message of peace.

She told others that hatred could only be overcome with love. She did not buy anything. When she was tired, she lay down on the earth and slept. When she was hungry, she fasted until she was offered food, but Peace Pilgrim never starved. People reached out with their compassion for this gentle elder with her kind message. She was treated like a queen by both wealthy and impoverished families along her path, and was given hospitality in exchange for her sweetness and kindness. Truly, Peace Pilgrim is an extreme but beautiful example of one person who chose a path of compassion for herself. Now, you don't have to toss all your belongings and become a wanderer, but I hope you will find simple joy on your own personal path of your design.

Now that you've gotten started with the basic ideas of compassion, we'll investigate in depth how to live a lifestyle that aligns with those values as much as possible. Here you'll find some of the problematic issues that might plague a person trying to live a harm-free lifestyle. The more you explore lessening harm and the more you plan harmless activities, the more you'll run into some roadblocks against being virtuous and pious. Here, we will use spirituality to hone your critical perception of the world rather than to distract you from it. If religion is the opiate of the masses, as Karl Marx suggested, this book is the wrong pharmacy for the proletariat!

We live at the top of the food chain in the modern Western world. As privileged people, we naturally stand strong at the expense of those who toil beneath us, simply because they were born into a different race, country, economic strata, or other marginalized group. I'm not saying you have to feel guilty, and I'm not even asking you to be angry about this situation, although it's okay if you are. I *do* want you to spiritually confront the less stable parts of humanity, society, and global events rather than let them slide. Confrontation will look different to different people: for some it may mean meditation and prayer, while for others it may mean mindful action and activism. Think about how you would react as we take a tour through some big issues.

Surrendering Pride

Pride is another matter related to vanity, but it encompasses so much more. Pride can completely ruin relationships: we can refuse to make amends or admit any kind of wrongdoing. Pride is also the enemy of changing any life matters that should be altered to reduce the potential for harm. Pride is the devil that tells us we won't be the one to make a mistake or be unlucky enough to have an accident on the job or in the car. Pride tells us that it's okay to be lazy and disregard safety rules or equipment because "we know what we're doing," or to not brief our friends on the proper courses of action when introducing them to an activity that might have safety concerns. Pride causes us to think there's something special about us that makes us impervious to the safety concerns about texting and driving or drinking alcohol.

Pride rears its ugly head in many ways and is insidious, because pride exists even in people who might otherwise be decent. Everyone falls victim to pride in some area of life, even when other areas of life are met with gentle humility.

Dealing with your own pride and the pride of others is especially problematic because it can ignite like fire and dynamite when the pride of two people combines. Indeed, this is the stuff divorces are made of, and it is the reason a toddler can bring a full-grown adult to a standstill in a supermarket. Everyone involved in a relationship needs to deal with pride head-on if it is to thrive. That's why for this section I'd like to introduce a group problem-solving technique instead of an individualized activity that involves letting go of pride as its key component.

Consultation

The following is a spiritual problem-solving technique, originally drawn from the Baha'i faith, called "consultation." All spiritual groups must have problem-solving strategies of their own that deal with the special problem of pride in spiritual people. In my own spiritual practice, I'm lucky enough to have achieved a station in my worship group that is technically the highest leadership position. But that position is of course only illusory: a leader like me is only as strong as her ability to surrender her pride. After all, even though I've got the last say in all matters, the other members of my group can vote with their feet and leave the group if I became a prideful tyrant. For this reason I must always be mindful of the other elders in my group and indeed all members. The result resembles more of a consensus than a dictatorship, considering the need to keep the group together.

When performing a consultation, unity and consensus are also key. Several steps must be taken to solve problems among a group of equals. First, a prayer is said to establish a feeling of unity and a spirit of friendly problem-solving. The group can agree upon a known prayer, or one person can wing it if necessary. Next, the facts should be stated. Each person can contribute everything he or she knows about the situation, free of judgment or subjective supposition. Feelings are considered to be part of the facts but they should be stated as fact only by the people who have the feelings; no one should guess how another person feels.

Once all the facts are on the table, it's time for suggesting potential solutions for the problem, even if they are solutions that can be tried for only a short amount of time until the group reconvenes to reassess the situation. The relinquishment of pride really comes into play at this stage. As the solutions are brainstormed, each person releases ownership of their own potential solution to the problem. All solutions brainstormed are equal in the group's eyes. In fact, one person can give several solutions, each of which might be mutually exclusive. In this way, it doesn't become a roundtable of people arguing for their own points of view. Instead, consulting is a collective brainstorming session in which the group is united to find any possible solution to the problem.

When all ideas are exhausted, the group then examines them. Clarifying questions can be asked, and anyone can offer additions or piggyback ideas on other ideas. When the time comes, voting is done to try to establish a consensus. This can be easier than it sounds if it is agreed that the solution is only tried for a set period of time, like a week. In this way, even the more wild ideas can find a place in the world. When a unanimous decision is reached, the consultation is over and the entire group can celebrate its agreement, rather than one person being the winner.

Live and Let Live

The phrase "live and let live" was exemplified by an incident that occurred in World War I. A story emerged that German and British soldiers had stopped fighting as the winter holidays drew near, and they even exchanged gifts and shared food and drink with one another. They played games and forged friendships. After the holidays, it was back to business as usual, unfortunately. However, the "live and let live" anti-war sentiment persisted. As long as people's lives don't include injury to themselves or others, allow them to live out their lives in peace. This saying can be extended to other interactions with those who are different from us. Meanwhile, the "live" part of "live and let live" implies that one should focus on his or her own business first and foremost while still exercising humility, echoing the proactive interpretation of compassion. Go out there and *live* your life in a way that doesn't harm anyone. Only after your own needs are addressed should you also be mindful that you are letting others live up to their full potential. You aren't granted permission to ignore the suffering of others, but you also may not add to that suffering through judgment.

Gwen Thompson used "live and let live" in her spiritual poem in the couplet, "Live and let live, fairly take and fairly give." In this way, Thompson tied the idea to the concept of giving and taking, a metaphor for balance. The phrases "fairly take" and "fairly give" could also be two different ideas taken separately that result in a reduction of harm. We can agree that "fairly take" is a realistic rule; we don't assume that one should take nothing at all from the world. We allow concessions a person might need to take a fair share of income from a job well done. We agree that we must eat our fair share of food. Certainly consumer choices and lifestyle choices can be changed to allow for fairness. It is not reasonable to try to eliminate what is taken, but it is reasonable to be fair about it. And being fair doesn't necessarily mean you should compare yourself to others, although some people use other people as benchmarks to make the duty simpler. However, being fair means that the amount you take from this world should makes sense in your own mind and heart. The rest is between you and the divine.

A special note here is that, for some people, the act of receiving is challenging. They say that the three hardest phrases to say are: I love you, I'm sorry, and I need help. I'm very free with the first two, but I admit that I find it very difficult to ask for help. Also, when I receive a blessing in my life, I have to consciously think about integrating the gift into my life instead of rejecting it or setting it aside. For example, do you find it easy to take a compliment by simply saying thank you and allowing the blessing of the compliment to wash over you? Or do you immediately deflect the compliment and mitigate your ability to take it by saying "oh, it's nothing," or something similar? If so, you may be able to reduce harm to your self-esteem by graciously taking compliments, and minimize harm to your life by accepting gifts if they are given in free will and good spirit.

"Fairly give" encourages generosity up to a point—notice that it doesn't say "freely give." Be fair about what you give to the world. Giving should not cause you undue suffering, and you will need to use your own judgment here. Again like the surgeon's incision, a pain that heals, what looks like initial harm may actually be of benefit. I can't tell you how many times I've tried to talk myself out of a volunteer opportunity in the morning because my car is out of gas and gas is expensive or because the weather is cold. I know that if I brave the elements and other challenges that are potentially ruinous, the benefits are great and the threat of harm will evaporate. Consider how fairly taking and fairly giving could balance your life so you could live to the fullest *and* reduce harm to yourself and others.

Consumption and Consumerism

One of the most common messages we receive in the West about reducing harm to others is related to our consumer consumption rate and our culture of consumerism at large. Some people are privileged enough to consider and make major lifestyle changes, and those people often promote such lifestyle changes to everyone. Thus we hear their endless list of solutions: "Reduce, reuse, and recycle!" "Go vegan!" "Buy American!" The cacophony of instructions may seem overwhelming and also disconnected from the overall goal of reducing harm. The critical thinker rightfully asks, "How does this have anything to do with anything?" You don't have to guilt trip yourself into joining any kind of movement unless you truly believe it is the best way to achieve your goals. That said, consumerism is a valid worry, and many are in a good place in life to address the issue. This section is devoted to reducing harm through consumer choices. If this topic applies to you, read on. If not, skip to a section that holds your passion and speaks to your heart.

Cars

The effect of cars on the planet and on our fellow humans is an excellent case example for harm reduction, because the effects are so obvious. We know that they pollute the air with carbon dioxide among other chemicals. We know that they use limited fossil fuels and crowd our roadways. Nobody thinks that cars are good for the environment. Even auto makers advertise their models featuring reduced environmental impact via lower gas mileage. Cars are a necessary evil for many, however. I myself live in a rural area without public transit and often have to travel into town to work with clients. Many others must also travel for work because they live in a rural area, or in place where safe public transit is not available. If you're in a position to swap a car commute for one on bicycle or on foot, it's wonderful to do so. You'll eliminate your car from traffic jams, reduce the amount of limited resources taken from the earth, and contribute nothing to the pollutants released into the air. If possible, ride sharing is another option to reduce harm from cars. You can take the bus, carpool, or participate in a car-sharing program if one is available in your area. If you have the means, you can buy carbon offsets for the car trips and airplane flights you do take. I'm personally lucky enough to be able to afford a hybrid car, and fuel efficient cars can help offset some of the damage done by fossil fuels and pollution.

Again, don't be hard on yourself if your life right now makes car ownership the only realistic option, even if you're passionate about this issue. You can reduce your number of car trips and offer carpools whenever possible. Make sure your tires are properly inflated and your car is regularly maintained to save gas and reduce emissions. If it's not yet the time in your life to trade your car in for a lifestyle that consumes less fossil fuels and harms less with pollution, then bear in mind that another stage of your life may present a better opportunity for you. For example, you may be heading to a job or running kids to school right now in a way that makes a car-free life impossible. That's just fine; waiting until retirement is a possibility. Keep this patience in mind with your other attempts to live compassionately. At each stage in life we are forced to take more from the world in some ways and less in others. When you were an infant, all you could do was take what was given to you. As you gained power through your life stages, opportunities for spiritual growth and harm reduction were and will still be presented to you. The goal should be to have awareness of those opportunities and the will to take them as they are presented to you.

If your passion is to reduce harm caused by cars, perhaps the best thing you can do is join with other people who share your goals. This doesn't mean you need to spread an agenda or evangelize for your cause; many people working together can be more effective at working toward a solution to a harmful problem. You could organize a car sharing program or a major van pool system, or even work with your local politician to arrange for mass transit or bike sharing stations to be built in your region. The sky is the limit.

How do you know what to do? Consider what will reduce harm to people both in the short and the long term. And if matters ever seem confusing and you debate the issue within yourself at times, that's okay. Your work toward compassion is the leading edge of your spiritual growth, so it's not necessarily supposed to be easy.

Food

When you think of consumption, you might think of food. Food is a necessity. The food itself is consumed, and resources are consumed in the production and transport of the food. You can't stop consuming food, but you can change the way you purchase. Consider buying local, as well as avoiding processed or excessively packaged foods. Food is a rich source of ideologies, and some seem diametrically opposed, because consumerism tells us the more we purchase, the better. I've mentioned two such examples so far, so let's examine these for a moment to illuminate the logistical issues some families might have when trying to follow these ideologies.

The hundred-mile movement is built on the idea of reducing the harm caused by transporting food. Transporting food uses fossil fuels, causes pollution, can be the cause of unsustainable farming practices and unjust labor practices, and it can even cause harm to the ecosystem in some cases. Followers of this movement thus attempt to only consume food grown or produced within a hundred miles, which results in a lot of shopping at farmer's markets and possibly local farms. In some cases, it can also mean spending more money on food if local food is more costly. Buying local also can help small businesses and puts money back into your community.

The vegan movement is devoted to reducing harm to animals and harm through some unsustainable livestock farming practices by avoiding the consumption of animal products entirely. You may already see how these ideologies, though both well-meaning, may be nearly impossible to follow in some cases. It would be tough to be both a vegan and a follower of the hundred-mile movement if you lived in the extreme north of Canada unless your diet was comprised entirely of lichen.

There are countless other dietary choices designed to reduce harm. If you're not ready to become a member of the hundred-mile movement, try smaller changes. For example, if you eat meat, consider buying humanely raised and butchered meat. Look for smaller grocery stores in your area that are not part of major national chains; support those mom-and-pop businesses. You could choose to only buy organic food in order to reduce potentially harmful farming practices. Or you could choose to only purchase fair trade food to reduce the harm caused by unfair labor and wage practices. Another option is to focus on avoiding self-harm by only purchasing food that is low in fat, cholesterol, sugar, or carbohydrates. In some cases, the matter of which foods cause harm to the self or the environment is still up for debate.

It's easy to get caught up in wondering which one is "right" instead of doing the intellectual work of thinking about daily choices. If one works for your lifestyle and makes you feel like you're on the right track, that's okay. However, sticking with food ideologies can also reach a pathological level. In fact, the American Psychological Association has identified a disorder called orthorexia, in which sufferers are so concerned with eating healthy, "good," and virtuous foods, that their physical health and relationships can actually suffer adverse effects.

How much your food choices harm your own life requires some soul-searching. It's not the goal of my writing here for you to reduce harm to others at the expense of your own safety and well-being. Instead, seek balance. Again, this may not be the life stage at which you can afford your ideal food, but later in life you may be able to buy what you want or grow your own food. Think of the long-term practicality of your choices, and try living life day to day. An all-or-nothing approach may be harmful in the case of food; even dieters have cheat days. If you are planning a major lifestyle change, even tiny tweaks can have a big effect over time. Try swapping just one ingredient you use daily for something you prefer and that you hope reduces harm in the world. Again, you can join together with others to make small efforts go farther. For example, you can start a pea patch community garden in your own neighborhood.

Clothes

When you think of consumerism, do you think about the clothes you wear? Even if you don't buy the name or designer brands advertised everywhere, clothes are still a "consumable" in that we continue to buy replacement clothes throughout our lives. I gave little thought to where my clothes came from until my kids accidentally brought it to my attention. Every day, my kids and I do an activity where we pray for a country on a world map. We go through the countries alphabetically so the kids learn to have concern for people in faraway places and at the same time absorb some knowledge of geography. When reading their clothing tags, I noticed I could quiz them on country names to find out if they recognized them from previous world prayer activities. I was fascinated by how many countries were represented on our family's clothing tags. Sadly, however, I learned that some of these clothing production locations have poor labor and wage practices.

Supporting slave-free practices is one way people can try to reduce harm through their clothing choices. Again, the clothing industry is another area in which ideology can take hold. Some people choose to only purchase clothes made in the USA, where fair labor laws and child labor prevention is practiced. You could choose to buy clothing made of bamboo or hemp in order to reduce the effects of cotton farming and polymer production on the environment. An affordable option is to buy clothes second-hand at thrift stores so that you aren't contributing to unethical clothing practices. As an added bonus, many thrift stores also support a local charity cause. You can also make further connections by refusing to support companies that you believe fund harmful political goals or harmful beauty standards.

As with other consumption habits, you'll need to pick your battles. Decide which of the following values, if any, call to you the most: reducing environmental harm, reducing harmful labor practices, or reducing societal harm. Decide how you can support your goals without harming yourself by inflating your budget to a degree that is impractical. You might be able to consider buying clothes produced locally, shop at thrift stores, or you might start up a clothes swap with friends. A piecemeal approach may work best for your lifestyle, as with other big changes. If even some of your clothing comes from a neighborhood swap or a thrift store, you are steering your financial support away from the systems that may be of concern to you. Over time, that can have a big effect. Notice how you can unobtrusively spread your practices to others without forcing ideology on them or making them feel guilty. Instead of talking them into embracing your goals, you can simply gift friends and family with locally made, hemp, or bamboo clothing or whatever suits your preferences around the holidays.

Trash

As a small child, I was passionate about eliminating litter at all costs. Indeed, my own children want to pick up litter as well; they want to protect the environment. It's probably one of the first ideologies about harm reduction I adopted in life, and it has stuck with me to this day. The trash that ends up in my garbage can is taken to a landfill that is only a few miles away, where it will stay for eons, leaching into the environment. My local garbage trucks have signs on them proclaiming that over half of their contents could have been recycled—talk about a guilt trip! Every time I threw an empty toilet paper roll into the bathroom garbage can instead of composting or recycling, it would come back to haunt me. Trash is a huge problem for the environment, so those who are passionate about reducing harm toward our Mother Earth are particularly drawn to this issue.

Trash gets to the root of the consumption issue. The more we consume, the more waste we produce. If this issue speaks to you, there are many practical ways to handle the garbage that leaves your home. We've all heard the rule of "reduce, reuse, recycle." Reduction of consumption is the first step. If you want to buy a new product, is there a way to buy it used and thereby reduce the number of products manufactured to fill the demand? You may even be able to find things free by joining a "buy nothing" or freecycle group in your neighborhood, or by organizing your own group. The Internet has given us plenty of new ways to acquire free things through social networking or free classified ads. You can also buy secondhand or refurbished merchandise. Even at the grocery store you can choose products that have reduced packaging. You can also buy bulk goods for refillable containers.

Reuse or repurpose your items until they're worn out and you're ready for new ones. You can rinse out containers and even baggies, and save items for crafts. Be sure that you're actually going to reuse the things that you save, however. There's no sense accumulating clutter if you're never actually going to use an item again. The trash sitting in your house is not much better for the environment than if it were sitting in a landfill. You may be able to find someone who will reuse some things you own, such as a crafter who loves old wire hangers, or a quilter who wants old fabrics to use. But don't keep them around out of the hopes that someday you'll find someone to take it off your hands. An overly cluttered home can become harmful to you and your relationships. It is enough to try reusing and recycling items to eliminate how much is thrown out.

There's not much that needs to be said about recycling. If it is available in your area, you're probably taking advantage of it already. It may only take extra effort to seek out local recycling opportunities for electronics, automobiles, motor oil, major appliances, and other odds and ends. In the home where I grew up, recycling was not available, but when I moved out and went off to college, I started a recycling program in our dorms when it wasn't yet available there. I had received so much information and encouragement as a child, there was no way I was going to miss out on recycling as an adult. If recycling is a passion of yours, there are plenty of ways to become crafty with reused objects and recycle them yourself to make interesting hand-made gifts. Of course ecological concerns can be expanded to include energy conservation and any number of related activities.

It will always be impractical to do all possible harm reduction strategies. Whatever is not right for you can be offset with something else you believe is more doable. Imagine that you were put on this earth to express the unique ideas that only you can have for harming none. It is your duty to love that life, not anyone else's.

The Beautiful and Unending Cycle of Compassion

Compassion isn't just one moment in time. You can't earn your trophy in compassion and set it on your shelf. Considering others with every action is a cycle that must be repeated throughout your path. Thinking about the harm that the average human life visits on the world is a very uncomfortable process. It can also be a tiring process if you don't properly manage the emotions associated with it. There's no single perfect ideology that fits everyone. So, every day, we must wake up and consider each action, from the work we choose to do throughout the day to the words we say to friends, family, and strangers. There are a seemingly endless number of choice-points in your life in which you'll have to consider the possibilities for harm, weigh and balance your own practical issues, and make a conscientious choice. Sometimes you'll make the wrong choice and that's okay. Other times you'll make the right choice but fail in its execution. That's okay, too. You're in the rock tumbler that is life, being polished until your jagged edges are smooth.

A study showed that being vigilant about mindfulness might actually cause you to be less exhausted by the idea of being compassionate for others. This study about "compassion fatigue" showed that greater mindfulness positively correlated with greater than average compassion satisfaction (Decker et al., 28). That means that the more the study's subjects practiced compassion, the easier the practice felt for them.

But when sorting through the minutiae of life and their potential harm on the world, how do we keep motivation strong? I'd like to offer another analogy. Keeping up a spiritual discipline like compassionate living in a messy world is like keeping a clean house with a messy family. Every day you have to repeat the same routines. When I clean my house, I have to sweep the floor every day. The next day, the floor is so covered with dirt from kids and pets that it looks like I never swept at all. Even my husband exasperatedly says, "Why should I sweep? It just gets dirty again." It's easy to see how attitude can make the difference between a soul-sucking chore and a healthy life routine. If I catch myself thinking about the inevitability of future dirt or feel resentful while sweeping, I change the tune of my thoughts. Instead, I try to make the action a loving act of care and prayer, which makes housekeeping become more bearable. Making it a loving act can also have a more positive effect on my life than simply having a tidy home.

Think of all the mental gymnastics you're doing to be compassionate as a sort of spiritual housekeeping for your soul. Yes, it is repetitive and maddening at times, but don't be discouraged. You are affecting the world around you, and you're also developing a discipline within yourself. All the hard work is worth it. You're developing a sense of character that is full of virtue. Consider your personal virtues as a touchstone. After all, compassion is an attempt to lead a virtuous life. A virtue needn't lead to pride or self-righteousness; virtues are something that even the humblest person can and should develop as they move through lessons big and small in life's spiritual journey.

Reverence

This virtue has to be at the top of the list. And choosing a personal goal to be compassionate is an excellent way to attune yourself with this value. Life is all fun and games until someone gets hurt, so if we focus on keeping ourselves and each other out of harm's way, our demeanor is more serious. There's no problem with having fun in life as well, but it should be balanced with a sense of what constitutes a serious duty, a serious responsibility, and what should be honored as sacred.

In my personal spiritual circles, my friends and I have a reputation for being traditionalists. We're adults who have come to value the tried and true rituals and the smells and bells that remind us what we're doing has worked before. As a result, people on the outside looking in might assume that we're stuffy, pretentious sticks in the mud. Nothing could be further from the truth! Even when we're praying and worshipping, we still make jokes and the temple rings with laughter as much as it does sacred songs and chants. This balance itself is something sacred, and it can be found in any spiritual path or even beliefs and practices that have no label at all.

It is easy to balance silliness with reverence in the company of good friends because you know when the other person needs a somber face and a hug and when to giggle instead. If you're on your own, your own mind will try to get the better of you. In times when you should be reverent and thinking through potential consequences, your own psychology may fight against having to picture a worst-case scenario. Other times, you might find that your spiritual practice gets too serious. The mirth is gone and you lose your sense of joy. It's especially tough to keep a light-hearted attitude when trying to carry out a spiritual duty to be compassionate. Try this simple exercise to balance your joy and reverence. It is a prayer and meditation that can be used on others and yourself.

Serious Wishes, Silly Wishes

Find a place and a time where you will not be disturbed. The place should be where you will feel comfortable meditating and praying out loud. Seat yourself comfortably and close your eyes. Pick a person from your prayer list. Beginners might find it easier to pick someone other than yourself at first. Generous people sometimes feel self-conscious praying for good things for themselves, but once you've got the knack of this exercise, I suggest trying it on yourself. Start with a prayer for protection for the person on your prayer list. Think about all of the challenges that he or she is dealing with in life right now that could potentially be harmful to body, mind, or spirit. Visualize this person strongly in your mind's eye. See his or her face, and try to feel emotionally as if you were in his or her presence. Here's an example prayer to be spoken aloud:

> Serious wishes for _____, from me to you.
> Protection from _____, strong and true.
> With harm to none, for the highest good
> This wish is done as it should.

The wording allows your protection to work in whatever manner is best for the person and for the universe without causing harm. Visualize the person surrounded by your protective love. You can think of this symbolically as a bubble of light, a person wrapped in a warm scarf of love, or you can simply visualize the person healthy and happy at home. Try to be nonspecific about how the person's problems will be solved so you don't have to think through the iterations of what could potentially cause harm. For example, when praying for an alcoholic to be safe from bad choices, it might be tempting to imagine him throwing down the bottle for good. But you don't know whether that choice might cause serious withdrawal symptoms and whether he really requires a safe, supervised medical detox. The best outcome may not arise from any action you imagine, so it is best to leave the manner and mode of protection up to the divine, the universe, or your preferred higher source or power out there.

For the second, silly part of the prayer, visualize something nice happening to the person. Remember the proactive version of the harm none rule: "do what you will." Visualize something wonderful happening for the person that would be totally harmless. It's okay to get specific with this visualization because you're allowed to cut loose and be silly as long as it doesn't cause hurt. Perhaps you'd like this person to win the lottery, write a hit song, or find the best Halloween costume ever. Even if your silly wish doesn't come true precisely, the positive vibes sent that person's way will do them and your heart good. Try some prayer wording such as this:

It's time for silly wishes for me to say,
I wish for _____ for you today!
With harm to none, for the highest good
This wish too is done as it should.

You can move on to another person on your prayer list, if you wish, or do this exercise again on another day. It is meant to uplift your spirits. Allow yourself to shift smoothly from meditating on someone's protection to imagining some wonderful blessings that make you smile. Learning to shift gears from serious to silly and then back again can help your spiritual practice tremendously, and it can give you an incentive to continue thinking about situations that need your attention even when there's serious thinking to be done.

Knowledge

Thoughts are things. Everything you think becomes reality, in a sense, within your conscious mind. You can then manifest a reality and effect change in the world through energy and action. The spiritual explanation for this is called the magical law of knowledge. If you know the true nature and the true name of a thing, you have spiritual power over it. The law can be exercised in prayer or other spiritual exercises to connect closely with the thing or person that you wish to influence. In everyday reality, knowledge is still incredibly powerful, which is why education for all is so important. The more you're educated about a particular topic, the more you can be empowered to prevent harm as it relates to that topic.

Here's where we run into a bit of trouble in this age of information: now that we have the Internet and every question can be searched in an instant, it's easy to only find information that confirms what you hope is true, a principle known as confirmation bias. If you want to find out if something is safe and harmless, it may not be sufficient to search on the Internet to find an answer. A large number of people have most likely made the same search with the same vested hopes for safety. People who are not experts on the topic can write about safety at length, weighting the issue with their bias. Even websites with lengthy bibliographies could be citing sources improperly or selecting only bits that support their argument. It's easy to learn just enough to be dangerous. Unless you've been trained to read scholarly studies, you might end up misinformed, even when you have the best of intentions.

So how does a person find information about compassion? As with everything, there are two approaches, practical and spiritual. Above all, know that you can't know everything about everything. You'll have to take a reasonable approach toward risk by consulting experts whenever possible. In other words, when worried about physical harm, talk to a doctor. They can help with many questions ranging from which car seats to use for children to whether it's safe for you to run a marathon. Likewise, you'll have to be resourceful and look for licensed, well-reviewed professionals in any category for which you'd like expert advice on harm reduction. Risk of legal harm? Consult a lawyer. Risk of financial harm? Consult a financial planner. And so on. It's certainly more expensive than searching online, but you can consider it a worthy part of your harm reduction discipline. Consulting an expert is considerably cheaper than going to medical school or law school, and it's much cheaper than what might result from illegal, uninformed, or unsafe decisions.

The spiritual approach to knowing is not to be confused with the intellectual way of knowing. *Intuition* is the word we have for the sense of knowing the truth about something without external evidence. Everyone has intuition; it's not a special magic power gifted to only a few people. However, many people learn to ignore their intuition if using it is not encouraged in their lives. Many more simply don't work to develop it. As a child, I was lucky enough to have parents who supported my desire to work on my intuitive skills. They bought me dream journals and divination tools to use to make intuitive predictions. So many other people aren't as lucky; they may have people around them who tell them to focus on the present instead of the future, and who denigrate intuition as silly. However, respectful intellectual-ism and spirit don't have to be at odds in anyone's life. Both can be used hand in hand to determine what is harmful in the world and what is not. Intuition and spirit are not replacements for scientific fact, but they are certainly good supplements.

Tomorrow, my four-year-old daughter has to go to the hospital for some minor surgery. It's the first time one of my kids will have such a procedure, so naturally I'm a nervous wreck. My entire brain is on fire with the desire to prevent harm to my beloved child. In this case, I've already turned to science and am allowing qualified doctors to care for her in a hospital setting. There's nothing more I can really do on the practical front. That's all in the competent hands of the professionals. In addition, I can intuitively turn to spiritual methods of harm prevention: I can calm my own emotional suffering by focusing on my intuitive sense that my daughter will be okay. I can also help both myself and potentially my daughter by praying for a safe surgery and healing.

If you are starting to get in touch with your intuition, you may need to practice some basics. Learning how to meditate quietly is one way to make room, space, and silence for perceptions that come from spiritual sources. For some people, intuition might feel emotional, like a sense of fear or anxiety that does not have any external explanation. Note that if any negative intuitions are prolonged, severe, or frequent, they could be signs of a mental health issue, and the issue might have to be managed medically. Occasional intuitive feelings of fear or anxiety should be acknowledged, especially if sensed during a time of meditation set aside for sensing potential sources of harm.

Intuition about potential harm might come as a positive emotional feeling as well, as a confirmation that the topic of your meditation is potentially harmless. For example, after asking your intuitive self whether it's a good idea to take tai chi lessons, you might feel a rush of peaceful well-being, happiness or ethereal joy. Those feelings could be considered personal confirmation for you.

For some people, intuition does not come as an emotion, but the message may come through in other subtle ways. Some people are very visual, so they may see pictures in their mind's eye, like in a daydream. The picture might be a confirmation vision, such as when people see themselves happy and safe, or they may see a symbol like a heart. The visual message may also come as a warning, such as seeing harm befall someone or a symbol like a bandage or a stop sign. The visual aspect is why it is important to close your eyes during meditation if you're trying to pay attention to your intuition.

It's also possible to hear a message, in the same way you might "hear" a song that is stuck in your head. You might receive the message of pleasant or abrasive music as a positive or negative answer to a meditative question. Words and phrases might come through directly, taking the guesswork out of the interpretation.

There are many ways to receive intuitive messages, like tactile sensations (chills or warmth) and even scents and tastes. Our bodies and minds are unique, so you'll have to take your own intuition for a test drive and get acquainted with how it works for you. And the best way to start is meditation.

Silent, Receptive Meditation Exercise

To try silent, receptive meditation, make sure you are free of distractions. Have a timer handy so you won't be tempted to keep checking the clock, and keep a piece of paper and a writing implement on hand so you can write down any impressions you get. Lock the doors, turn off any distracting electronics, and dim the lights. Settle yourself in a position that is comfortable. It is okay if you accidentally fall asleep, but you can avoid that by meditating during a time of day when you feel alert. If you're new to meditation, set your timer for a short period of time, like five minutes. If you're old hat at meditation, try it using your intuition about compassion for at least twenty minutes a day to get in the habit and give yourself an opportunity to receive messages about this topic.

Step 1) Before starting your meditation, state your intention clearly to yourself. For example, say "I intend to receive messages about how I can be more harmless today," or ask, "Should I write a song for my friend?" Or you can say, "Will this gift cause no hard feelings or any other harm?" You can be either general or specific.

Step 2) When beginning your meditation, try to let go of your conscious thoughts. If you "hear" a running monologue about your surroundings or your day, gently remind yourself that you're meditating by releasing those thoughts. Try to observe them as if they were someone else's thoughts and then return to clearing your mind. It is okay if you are distracted frequently by your own thoughts at first. It takes time and practice to become skilled at meditation, but it does get easier if you stick with frequent meditation sessions.

Step 3) When the time is up, write down any impressions you received. You can also sketch visual messages. Write down how you feel after meditating, as well. If you received no impressions, make a note of it. It may be that you need more practice or your meditation sessions should be lengthened.

Daring

Try new things and be innovative about your compassion practice. It may seem odd that I'm promoting daring as a virtue, but wanting to live with compassion doesn't mean that you should stay in bed wrapped in bubble-wrap all day so that you don't inflict yourself on the world. You must experiment, make mistakes, and generally work toward improvement. Don't let yourself fall into a rut carved by anxiety. Fear of harming yourself and others is natural and healthy, and that fear should compel you to be mindful without dampening your spirit and zest for life. Hope for each new day should outweigh any fears.

How should the conscientious person become more daring? Cultivate a proactive sense that says "get out there and harm none." You can make your life more about doing things than avoiding things. Try this exercise. Right before going to sleep, allow yourself to fantasize about the day ahead. Picture everything going swimmingly. Think up activities you could do that would not cause any harm, and imagine those ideas being executed flawlessly. For example, if you thought of handing out food to the homeless, imagine seeing the happy faces of the volunteers who coordinate donations. The homeless are having hard times, and your act of kindness has made someone's day more survivable. If you thought of taking a walk in a wooded area, imagine ideal weather and chirping birds. These are the perfect visions of your plans, and they don't have to exactly match reality. Instead, you're painting these positive pictures to help yourself perceive the best in things instead of talking yourself out of perfectly fine activities.

Recall the law of attraction: the more you visualize good things happening in your life, the more these things will happen. Like attracts like. When you think positive thoughts, positive energies and events will come to you. Conversely, if you fill your mind with negative thoughts, negative energy will affect your life. You can see how even the pragmatist who believes in the law of attraction would not want to spend much time thinking about harmful things that could come about from actions. Realistically, I advise seeking balance. You will have to allow yourself to play out harmful acts to their inevitable conclusions in your mind if you need to convince yourself not to do them. I often play out a conversation with my husband or my kids in my head before I start it, just to make sure I'm not picking a fight. If you see the harm that can come of an action, you can choose not to carry it out and dismiss the thought from your mind. There's no need to ruminate over negativity. However, there's no harm in letting yourself daydream positive flights of fancy. In fact, there may be some good that comes of it.

Justice

Justice is an interesting concept. Like love, it is a powerful truth for many that is known in the heart and mind rather than made through natural observations. In the courts, people present evidence in pursuit of justice. However, evidence can be interpreted by different people in different ways. Some believe that people who do harm should be harmed in return. Some people believe that especially egregious harms, like child or animal abuse, should be answered with more severe punishments than the harm inflicted. And still others believe that punishment in all forms is folly, and that only kindness and love can rid the world of all harm, rather than continuing a vicious cycle.

I'm not going to tell you what to believe with regard to justice, but you should start thinking about it, since it may affect how you approach compassion. Consider now, what is your concept of justice? Is punishment necessary for criminals? For naughty children or pets? Does anyone deserve harm? Would it be okay for you to harm somebody who has harmed you or others? Would it be okay for somebody to harm you if you had harmed that person or someone he or she loves? You may be able to think of some circumstances that make you answer these questions one way, and other circumstances that result in the opposite conclusion. That's okay; there may not be one hard and fast rule for you.

A sense of justice can differ among people, and that's one thing that makes the idea of compassion so difficult. Try not to focus on an external sense of justice, but instead examine how your own affects your life. For example, do you feel the need to punish yourself or mope and feel guilty after you've made a mistake that resulted in harm? Think about whether this pattern is helpful or harmful in your own life. It could be that the temporary bad feeling helps you integrate the lesson you learned into your life, letting you spring back into action. Or, it could be that this cycle of self-punishment cripples your ability to be positive and proactive. If the latter case is true, you may have to work to be gentler on yourself. If self-punishment is a pervasive problem, it may be helpful to work with a therapist to understand what triggers these thoughts and actions, and if there are more productive alternatives.

Again, these elements are all very subjective, and there's no one-size-fits-all rule for justice in life. There are, however, ways you can band together with other proactive people to promote social justice, if that is a passion of yours. There are opportunities for volunteering locally and abroad. There is also the option to simply make art or create dialogue and express your own views of justice to other people. Finding others who share your sense of justice can be comforting, and together you may be able to come up with ideas and actions that can better the world.

Looking for Crossroads in Your Life

Another way to be proactive is to constantly be looking for ways to give your life a positive overhaul. Spring cleaning? Perhaps you've got an opportunity to donate things to people in need. Car totaled? Instead of buying the same make and model, it might be time to look for one that is more fuel efficient or investigate other modes of transportation. Lost your job? Perhaps you can find a job that aligns better with your values. Relationship ended? Maybe your next love match will share more of your goals. Major crossroads in life are stressful because they require great change. Looking at these major life change points as opportunities for living your beliefs more deeply will help you get through transitions.

Take a moment to look forward at any upcoming major life changes. Perhaps you're planning to graduate from school and look for a job, to get married and move, or to return to work after small children go off to school. Whatever your plans may be, think about how you can begin searching for opportunities to reduce harm in the world through your newly created lifestyle. Now is the time to have some of those positive daydreams. Imagine how your life will look afterward if everything works out in the ideal way.

Don't limit thinking about your positive hopes for the future to when you're about to fall asleep. You can plan a more beautiful future any time. Here's another opportunity to make a vision board, the process for which is described in chapter 2. You can use visual representations of things you hope to bring about in the world, or images that show what you'd like the world to look like. Again, clip pictures from magazines and glue them to make a collage of your hopes and dreams. Also remember to visualize the final successful view of your goals rather than the ways of getting there. Doing so frees up the method of execution, and the mysterious forces of the universe can sort it out properly. You can also make a virtual vision board online or collect images in a folder on your computer. The trick is viewing your vision board often. Post it in a place where you will look at the pictures frequently and feel happy. The positive emotions from viewing your vision board should radiate outward into your life, creating the chain reaction necessary to build your dreams.

five

Becoming a Beacon of Kindness for Others

After you've integrated compassion into your lifestyle from all avenues, you're likely to want to spread the message to others or at least encourage them to try the same. It's tough to be a peaceful person who greets everyone with open arms if you are faced with opponents armed with weapons of war. Be kind to others, even when they are jerks. When more people adopt a compassionate lifestyle, everyone benefits. Less harm in the world means that harm is less likely to befall you or a loved one. Accidental harm will always be with us as a species, of course, but the greatest enemy in attempting to get folks to agree to love one another is a difference in ideology.

Even among those who agree that kindness is best, there may always be a difference in opinion on how best to bring it about. For instance, some people believe in disarmament while others believe that an armed society is a polite society. Some people believe that Western medicine is safe and relieves harm, while others believe it is toxic and harmful in comparison with natural medicine. It will certainly be impossible to get everyone to agree tomorrow on the means to live harmlessly; world peace is not likely to be on tonight's news. However, that doesn't mean that we can't strive toward the ideal, just as we've done throughout these pages. It is necessary to do so in a way that is not oppressive or subversive. Pushing any one ideology would be rash and counterproductive.

Accusatory or negative messages only cause other people to withdraw and defend. Instead, we'll concentrate on spreading the message of compassion with the same gentleness and self-exploration with which these ideas were introduced. We'll investigate some of the issues that make our society reticent about spreading the message of compassion so that we can each strive to find avenues to reach others. If only one of us succeeds, we can all succeed.

Some virtues will also make appearances in others in the course of our grand quest. Chief among these may be the virtues of gentleness and practicality. Every small step toward reducing harm can be made great by greater numbers: lots of practical solutions implemented by lots of people.

Banding together is important. After reading, you may even be inspired to pursue great political goals. Remember that the deepest spiritual work often spreads first from the self to those closest to us, where we live and work. You are encouraged to reach out and embrace the ones close to you, even if you must deal with characters who are greedy, foolish, proud, or exhibit other distasteful behavior.

Compassion is a message that is meant to be shared—it does not exist in a vacuum. It exists as an ideal in relationships, societies, and global communities. Perhaps the divine message of compassion was given for a reason beyond the preservation of life. It may have been to bring attention to the struggle to share its message, that everyone is called to agree on its practical implementation. There's something magical about the problem, isn't there? It seems unsolvable, yet it must be endured, puzzled over, and ultimately unlocked.

Individualism Teaches Us Self Above Others

Before moving forward with spreading a lifestyle and philosophy of harm prevention and harm reduction, it's important to know what barriers you'll be working against. Chief among these may society's mindset. In Western culture, we've been taught since the day we were born to be individuals rather than work closely with others, avoiding harm at all costs.

As babies, my neighbors and I were placed in our own cribs, some of us in our own rooms. We were encouraged to play independently as infants rather than only interact with our parents and siblings. As soon as we could hold a spoon, we were encouraged to feed ourselves no matter the mess that resulted. In cultures not as individualistic as our own, it would seem silly to allow a baby to make a mess instead of using feeding time as an opportunity to practice cooperation and community over individuality.

Don't mistake my meaning; I don't think individualism is wrong. I'm raising my children to express their individuality in very much the same way I was raised. Individualism is part of our culture in the US. But that same individualism causes people to think of themselves as separate from family and friends and neighbors. This way of thinking can certainly be beneficial in a society where we have to work for a living and form new relationships, but it means that things like empathy, sympathy, and compassion must be explicitly taught. It won't likely be absorbed simply by being around already harmless people. Yes, it is important to be a good example, but you'll also have to have some uncomfortable conversations if you want to get the message any further than the end of your own nose.

I wrote in chapter 1 a bit about what to do if you have too much empathy. Now, I'd like to talk a little bit about what to do if you don't have enough, or if you're dealing with a person who doesn't seem to experience it at all. Remember, as with all major life changes, the person should want to make the change before change is attempted. Otherwise you'll be fighting a battle the whole time, and *that* may be counter to the goal of compassion. Once the person agrees, the next step would be to give instructions on how to experience the feelings of others.

Partnered Empathy Exercise

Sympathy for another can be gained by imagining that the suffering person is a loved one or a child. Empathy is a little more intense because you are feeling the suffering as if you were suffering yourself. For that reason, I will give you tools to avoid overlaying the real suffering onto yourself, as it may feel too great for you to handle. Empathy is still a worthwhile power to have, so this exercise will be a gentle way to tune in to it authentically.

Ideally, this exercise should be performed with the person for whom you want to feel empathy. If someone in your life is suffering, you can invite him or her to do this exercise with you. However, any person can recall a moment in life when he or she felt suffering to feel this exercise. For example, if you know someone who experienced the death of a loved one, you can ask the person to recall the death in order to experience the sadness, but only if he or she is comfortable doing so. Another note: before you do this exercise, read through grounding and shielding methods in chapter 3 again.

With your empathy partner, find a comfortable and private space where the two of you won't be disturbed. Privacy may be important. One or both of you could end up in tears, which is embarrassing for some people. You don't want to add embarrassment to the tide of emotions. Sit facing the person, and ground yourself thoroughly. You don't want to shield yourself yet, but if you feel overwhelmed by emotion you may want to ground yourself again and then shield yourself as a protective measure. You can offer to read through the grounding section with your partner as well, since the practice may be helpful. If you'd like to have grounding on hand, it may be helpful to have a rock to hold and a bit of salt to put on the tongue.

When thoroughly grounded, ask your partner to allow him- or herself to feel the emotion only to the extent that is comfortable. Look at your partner's eyes and allow yourself to examine his or her face for emotional cues. Ask yourself what he or she is feeling. Look for all the cues. Is there a widening or narrowing of the eyes? What happens with his or her eye contact? Watch the corners of the mouth and the slope of the shoulders. Is there any body language with the person's feet, hands, or general posture? Take it all in and try to get a bead on the nature and full extent of the emotion the other person is feeling.

If both of you are still feeling emotionally comfortable, ask if you can hold the person's hands. Once holding his or her hands, pay attention to the feeling between you two. You may sense energy flowing as a warmth, a coolness, a prickling, or a fuzzy sensation. Hold this position for a few moments and wait to feel the emotion. Your empathy might feel like you're legitimately feeling the emotion of the other person. Or it could feel like a sense of tiredness, anxiety, or a change in temperature or pressure. When finished, withdraw your hands and thank the other person. Then ground yourself again. You can offer for the other person to go through the grounding process with you. Touching the rock or putting a bit of salt on the tongue can be done at this time to aid grounding if either of you is feeling overly emotional from the experience. If need be, you can shield yourself at this time.

If you want another person to share empathy with you or with another person, you can help them through this experience. I've led my preschooler through this, but it could certainly be done with an adult. When she's hurt her brother's feelings, I say to my daughter, "Look at his face. What do you suppose he's feeling? Why?" These questions help lead her through the experience. Giving him a hug allows her to apologize in her own way as well as exchange energy to feel empathy. These exercises are basic in nature, but they are necessary to allow people in an individualistic society to learn empathy, then sympathy, and finally compassion.

Kind Eyes Group Exercise

This is a group exercise that taught me how to start showing compassion to strangers with just a simple smile and kind eyes. Reading through this exercise, it might sound silly to you, but it was a life-changing experience for me when I first practiced it with new schoolteachers at an art retreat. This group exercise is a perfect ice-breaker for prayer meetings, activism gatherings, family reunions, or any other group of compassion-minded people. The more participants, the merrier.

First, divide the group in half. Tell the participants that half of them will walk around the room or space clockwise, and the other half will walk around the room counter-clockwise. For the first five minutes of the exercise, each participant should try to make eye contact with as many people heading the opposite direction as possible. When each person makes eye contact, he or she should try to hold the eye contact as they pass and give a warm smile to the other person. Set a timer and start the exercise. There should be lots of giggles and smiles going on. Especially with a large group of strangers, it feels sort of fun and frantic to try to catch the eyes of so many unfamiliar people.

When the timer goes off, tell the group that they will walk around the room in the same way, but this time nobody should make eye contact with anyone. Set the timer for five minutes again and start the second part of the exercise. Participants will find that this phase of the exercise is familiar. Avoiding eye contact is what many people do every day, especially if they live busy lives in heavily populated areas. When I practiced this exercise, there was a sad part of my heart that found avoiding eye-contact eerily comfortable. There's a part of me that yearns for communities that recognize the humanity in all members. A first step toward creating that community may simply be to look into the eyes of those whose paths you cross.

Gentleness

The most important virtue to use when spreading any sort of message you'd like others to adopt of their own free will is gentleness. We've probably all been victims of pushy people from other belief systems trying to get us to follow their way of understanding the world. If you haven't experienced such a thing, I can tell you, it can be annoying at best. It sort of feels like you're standing ankle deep in refreshing ocean water while someone stands in the sand and shouts that you're drowning while throwing a life preserver at your head. The person means well, but you simply are not experiencing the same reality he or she seems to be experiencing. It's a problem of perception, and the frantic tone of the message being delivered does not help.

It's hard to control your emotions when you find something spiritually good; I can understand that. It's like seeing a beautiful sunset. You want to share it with someone and jump up and down, shouting at people to look. If you feel strongly about an ideology you've embraced that does not involve harm, the feeling will be intensified. It may seem like getting peoples' immediate attention is the only way to save the world, and that it has to be done quickly within your lifetime. The only problem is that other people feel just as strongly about completely different ideologies. We can't have them all happen at once.

The best way to be gentle is to allow people to make choices of their own free will and decide what is best for them and those around them, just as you carefully did while reading and working through exercises to this point. Keep in mind that most people really are good people; they're already trying to reduce harm as best they can while dealing with stressful problems and the needs of family, work, school, and more. A gentle touch with such folks is especially important to encourage actions they already do. When you see someone going the extra mile to be compassionate and kind, reach out in thanks.

When I was a new mom, I was once breastfeeding my baby in a hallway when somebody handed me a pre-printed card that said, "Breast is best for babies. Thank you for breastfeeding." This person had decided that harm was reduced to babies by breastfeeding and had chosen to do something about it by encouraging people who are breastfeeding in public. Of course, mothers and fathers who feed their babies formula are wonderful people too, and should not be shamed for their choice of baby food. But I found this act of gentleness surprising and effective. Even a controversial stance on reducing harm can be gently supported for those who already are making that choice. If you have a controversial idea of your own as to how harm may be reduced or eliminated in the world, this may be one plan of action you can use in a gentle way.

What if you want to confront somebody who is doing something harmful? This situation must be addressed as well, and it is possible to do so gently. Nonviolent communication is a technique taught in schools and used by counselors to teach couples and families how to speak with one another during conflicts. When using nonviolent communication, one must make the assumption that all human beings have needs and we're all just trying to get those needs fulfilled in the best ways we can. Unfortunately, fulfilling some needs can be done in harmful ways. For example, when a two-year-old throws a tantrum and hits his sister, he's not doing so out of some malicious will to be a harmful person. In fact, he may not yet even understand that punching his sister causes harm, believe it or not. Instead, he may be expressing a need for attention, a need to take a nap, or some other inherent human need. The need is not invalid, but it can be achieved in a different way than the harmful way he has chosen.

Nonviolent communication can be used to focus on expressing your own needs for harmless behaviors. When you express your needs, you take the spotlight off the person who is performing the harmful behaviors and put it on yourself, reducing the likelihood that the person will respond with defensiveness. You can do this with any harmful act by using this message format or something similar: "I feel _____ when you _____ because I need _____."

For example, imagine a situation in which a husband laughs lovingly at the way his wife's hair looks tousled in the morning. He's doing so not because he's malicious; he likes to feel a sense of playfulness with his wife. But she feels very hurt when this happens. If she were to declare, "You keep making fun of me. Stop it," he might rightfully become defensive, because he never thought of it as poking fun. A less harmful response would be, "I feel hurt when you laugh at me in the mornings, because I need to feel beautiful and comfortable with my body." This phrasing paints a fuller picture of her feelings and her needs. He could use this form too. "I feel love when you look beautiful but messy in the morning because I need to feel playful and happy with you." Both people can agree on a less harmful behavior. Perhaps she could suggest other times to be playful when she's less grumpy. Perhaps he could suggest less hurtful words to express his affection in the mornings. There may be no single solution to a problem, but they can arrive at something compassionately.

Dealing with Greed

Because everyone has needs, there's plenty of greed in the world today. Much harm can be caused by greed because people assume that their own values outweigh the potential for harm to others. You can see how that might be an easy assumption to make if someone has concrete values in life and is passionate about them. It's important to have compassion even for greedy people so you can approach them with gentleness instead of anger. At the same time, you'll also have to find the strength within yourself to be firm and unyielding so you won't suffer from the greed of others.

Many people reading here might tend to have very giving personalities. Over a lifetime, that personality type can attract greedy people who have no qualms about taking advantage of generosity or hospitality. If you're generous with your money, people will gladly take it. If you're generous with your personal space, time, and effort, people will fill your calendar with things to do. The tendency can be either to wait until you've run completely out of resources, or to become resentful until you explode at someone. Neither of these options are healthy and both are certainly harmful.

In the section on generosity in chapter 3, I wrote about how the best method for giving of yourself is to decide first how much you have in your budget to give. The same holds true for time and energy just as it does for money and material things.

But does it always work? Not really. I tend to give more of my time and energy than I should because I overestimate how much I can achieve in a given period of time. I also tend to allow others to ask me for favors or to show up early at my home and overstay their welcome because I don't want to be rude. Giving in to other peoples' greed can be harmful in the long run for all concerned. I could run out of time and energy to share with those who really need it. I have to allow space in my schedule for friends when they have emotional crises. And I must remember to leave room for unexpected problem solving sessions of my own.

Simply knowing that a greedy person needs to be confronted can be painful. Dreading the confrontation itself can cause personal harm. And once the person is confronted, he or she may feel hurt that you kept quiet about it for so long. It's important to deal with greed as soon as it becomes apparent. In this section, I'll provide some practical and spiritual techniques you can use to protect yourself from greed.

The first thing to do is reassess your needs: if you realize that greedy people are taking advantage of you or of a situation, then you have incorrectly assessed how much of a resource you have to give. Your budget is a little off, but that's okay. Now you can decide where to draw a line before confronting the greedy person or parties. Create a new budget that will give a little more to you. It may mean more free days on your calendar or more time to recharge yourself, for example.

You may need to spread time or resources to other people who are not getting enough. Be aware of how much of your personal resources you have to spare.

When you're ready to confront the greedy person, try nonviolent communication. Explain your feelings and tell the person the new needs that you have. For example, "I feel overextended when you come early and stay late on Sundays because I need time to have dinner alone with my husband. Can you make sure in the future that you arrive at six o'clock and depart by eight?"

If you find yourself repeatedly giving more of yourself than you should, you might want to try a spiritual exercise to protect your resources. The following meditative exercise is called a binding. The purpose in this case is to preserve or protect something or someone from being used. You'll need a skein of red yarn or a spool of red string and a picture or object that represents the resource you're trying to protect. For example, if you're giving too much of your time away, you can use an old, broken watch. If you're giving too much money away, you can use a dollar bill. You can also draw a picture of your resource if you like.

This exercise is best done at the waning moon, because the waning of the moon represents the waning of the behavior that you're trying to stop. As the moon disappears, so too will your problem with giving too much of your resources. Find a private spot where you can chant aloud without disturbing anyone, or be disturbed by anything. Place one end of the thread or yarn on the object that you've chosen for this exercise and focus your attention on what you're doing. You're going to wrap the object up with the thread or yarn until you've used up all the string you have. Here's a chant that you can use as you wrap:

What's mine I keep or free,
With my heart and with my head.
What I need is mine alone until I cut this thread.

When you are finished wrapping the object, tuck or tie the end of the string so that it won't become unraveled. Keep the object somewhere protected. You might want to place it somewhere as a reminder, such where you stash your money if giving money away has been a problem, or with your calendar if giving too much of your time away is a problem. If you want to be freer later with your resources, you can simply cut the thread and bury the object and thread.

Dealing with Ignorance

Very little is more frustrating than dealing with people who simply don't understand what harm they're inflicting on the world. Ignorance is often met with exasperation at best and rage at worst. It's especially difficult to be gentle when dealing with foolish people. But of course, there's nothing to be gained from yelling at an ignorant person. Their mind is not going to be changed by your or anyone's rants, and an angry person's behavior might even scare onlookers away from the right actions. In this section I'll again explain practical and spiritual ways to deal with ignorant and foolish people in your life.

When it comes down to it, you have two options: educate or walk away. Remember that when I refer to "foolish" or "ignorant" people, it means those who are harming others and not understanding the harm they cause. Now, I'm not suggesting you can't be friends with people who have learning or intellectual disabilities. Foolishness and ignorance in this context mean those who are unwilling to see the harm they cause. To those who refuse to be educated, it is important to protect yourself and others you care about by avoiding contact entirely.

If you choose to try to educate the person who is acting foolishly, do so gently. Prepare yourself with information before confronting the person. Use your nonviolent communication techniques to explain to the person how he or she makes you feel and needs you have that could be fulfilled. If the person seems unable to understand the problem, try helping him or her feel empathy. You can ask questions about how he or she would feel in that situation. You can't force somebody to feel empathy who doesn't want to do so, however. It could be that the person has natural energy shields he or she is using at full power to avoid feeling the harm of the situation.

If you reach the understanding that the person will never understand the harm he or she is inflicting on the lives of others, it may be your sad duty to cut the individual out of your life, which is often harder than it sounds. Whenever I am forced to do this, I have to delete the person's contact information from my computers, phone, and any other devices so I'm not tempted to send the person a message in a weak moment of nostalgia. It also requires being the bigger person and not trying to have the last word in the conversation. Let the other person's last message to you be the last, as you have no obligation to tell the person you're initiating a no-contact situation unless you truly believe it will help end the conversation permanently. That said, a foolish or ignorant person who harms others may be unlikely to respect your wishes to end contact. The best option may be to block the person entirely using what resources for privacy are available to you.

The hardest thing about trying to distance yourself from a harmful person is the battle that rages in your own mind. Therefore, I'd like to present to you an exercise you can do when you're ready to let someone go from your life. This exercise is best performed during the waning moon, as the disappearing of the moon represents the person disappearing from your life harmlessly and without fanfare.

Letting Someone Go

You'll need a safe place to burn paper items, so you'll need access to an outdoor fireplace or an indoor fireplace with a fire extinguisher handy. If you have no place to burn safely, an alternative exercise is to clip up the paper items into many small pieces and then recycle them. The fire or cutting and recycling represents the transformation of your relationship.

You'll need a photograph of the person you'd like to leave your life. It would be best if you can find a photo of the two of you together so you can cut the two of you apart. A drawing will do as well, if you don't have a photograph of the person. You can burn other paper mementos, too, such as letters or cards from the person, but be sure not to burn plastic or painted items, for safety's sake. Before performing the exercise, make sure you take the practical steps of deleting the person from all your contact lists so you won't be tempted to call or write to him or her.

When you're ready to perform the exercise, first allow yourself to think about any fond memories that you recall about the person. Allow time to relax and reminisce about happy things, even if there are many negative things about the relationship as well. Then, holding the paper item in your hand, visualize the person leaving your life happily and going on to do other good things. If it's a coworker, perhaps visualize him getting a much better job at another company. If it's a neighbor in an apartment complex, perhaps imagine her getting an opportunity to buy her first home and move happily into a new space away from you. Holding the vision in your mind, toss the papers into the fire or clip them up into tiny pieces. The exercise is complete. You have transformed the relationship into positive memories. You can now move on.

Dealing with Vanity

I'm going to discuss this quality and pride separately, although vanity is one expression of pride. Vanity is an excessive sense of pride in your own achievements or appearance, and it is one vice that many religions speak against. An inflated sense of self-importance and shallow admiration of oneself can cause one to believe that harm is an acceptable price for a good appearance. It's easy to confuse social status and outward appearance with well-being, as our society is materialistic to the point where people who do not own nice things and groom themselves nicely are thought to be lesser people. When trying to move upward socially in the workplace to earn money for survival, things like fancy clothes or cars or electronic devices may seem to be of great importance and value. Vain people can end up disregarding the feelings of others, or make choices that can be harmful to other living beings, the planet, or even themselves. Vanity can even be one cause of addiction to substances.

The ways vanity can be confronted differ if you're dealing with vanity in yourself or others. If you're dealing with your own vanity, you'll need to target some of the behaviors you know are a problem. For example, if you spend too much on makeup or appetizers and beers with friends after work, you can work on cutting back on your spending. Some people make it a New Year's resolution to cut back on such vices, tying their promise to a holiday. Others borrow from the religious tradition of Lent, quitting vices for the six weeks before Easter. One way I try to make myself a better person is to examine myself for self-improvement every full moon. I make a full moon vow to do something that will reduce my vain behavior in the month ahead, such as constantly posting my achievements to social networks. At the next full moon, I re-examine my goal and look at how well I've done. If I've shown improvement, I choose another goal. If I'm still struggling with that particular vain behavior, I make it my vow for the next full moon as well.

If you're dealing with the vanity in others that consistently causes harm, you will need to address the problems as they arise. You may start with some nonviolent communication so the person can see how their vain and self-centered behavior may be harming you or others. There's a good chance that the person has never thought about the consequences of selfish actions. It's possible that a low self-esteem or a need for acknowledgement and love is the root of their selfishness. Take a compassionate look at the person's life and see if there are some serious issues that need to be addressed. Offer a listening ear and ask if the person needs some help. Refer him or her to affordable counselors nearby if the person is suffering from addiction, low self-esteem, or an inability to form and keep relationships in a healthy way. You can also present alternative activities that will get the person's focus away from the harmful vain behaviors.

When I was a schoolteacher, I had to deal with a lot of good teenagers who often displayed harmful and vain behaviors. Of course, I couldn't blame them; they were all dealing with crises of self-esteem and in most cases, general self-identity. Teenagers strive for acknowledgement from their peers, and often deal with their first budding romantic relationships. It's hard to get them to look up from navel-gazing long enough to see that there are others who can be harmed by cruel words and reckless behavior. As a teacher, I sometimes played matchmaker with students and their passions. One vain kid was struggling with addictions and other self-destructive behaviors. I discovered he had a love of caring for younger children and playing chess, so I hatched a plan. I'll always remember how his self-centered focus shifted to others when he taught another kid a love of the game. It was evident again when he helped a kindergartener learn to read. This same strategy can be done with adults or even with yourself. The trick is to find a passion external to the self to draw your focus.

The divine and the spiritual world can be external to the self, and existing within the self, simultaneously. For that reason, spirituality is one cure for self-focus that allows you to love yourself at the same time. If you find yourself suffering from vanity, or causing others to suffer because of it, try pouring yourself into the spiritual pursuits of your choice. Covered now with the bandage of vanity, that divine-shaped hole within can be filled with your own understanding of spirit.

Rid Yourself of Vanity

Here's a spiritual exercise to help rid yourself of your own vain pursuits. You'll first need to do some soul searching to find where the source of your vanity lies. You can do that exploring with a counselor or it may be that you have a high degree of self-awareness already. Only you can decide. This exercise is designed for you to find three expressions of vanity in your life, but it is adaptable to a greater or lesser number. You'll need white rope or yarn measuring about three feet in length.

This exercise has two important parts to it, and both are best performed at the full moon. The fullness of the moon represents the maturity and power you'll need to acknowledge and fully own your vanity as well as to let go of any selfish vices that no longer serve you well.

Before you get started, settle on the number of vices you'd like to work on. (I can tell you from experience that there's nothing more annoying than finishing up a spiritual exercise like this and then realizing you've left out a really important one!) Next, think about each vain problem in turn, and tie a loose knot representing each one. When you've finished tying knots, survey your work and think about how these problems have served their time in your life and have been a part of you. When you are ready to release them, you can untie each one in turn and bury the rope. Keep in mind, you really need to be ready to let them go. You can leave the knots tied until New Year's Day, Lent,

the next full moon, your birthday, or whenever you feel ready
to stop being vain and selfish, and start moving toward a more
spiritual version of yourself.

Practical Advice

Everybody loves practical advice, at least when they're ready
for it. And so much the better if you can offer practical advice along with a helping hand. I'd like to share a story about
a time when I was really suffering, at least in a way that first
world problems allow me to suffer. I was taking a trip with
my newborn son. I had to travel across the country to fulfill
my doctoral program's residency requirement, and that meant
that I had to take my baby with me. He refused to drink from a
bottle, so it was impossible for me to leave him with his father
and big sister back at home.

Of course, I ended up being *that* person on the airplane
with the squalling baby. He wasn't hungry, but I'm sure his little
ears hurt from the change in air pressure. I was exhausted from
taking the lousy red eye flight I had booked before he was even
born. I paced up and down the aisle, receiving the deadliest, ici-
est glares from the other suffering passengers who were all wishing they could get some sleep. That's when the practical advice
miracle occurred, one that relieved us all.

A kind old woman caught me by the elbow as I walked
by her seat and said something I wasn't expecting. She asked,

"How can I help?" I looked up, my eyes brimming with tears and my brain fuzzy from new-mom lack of sleep. She leaned forward. "Would you like me to hold the baby for a while?" Nodding blankly, I handed over my son and high-tailed it to the bathroom. I had been suppressing the need to go for hours. Returning to her in a few moments, I felt refreshed and ready to rock my son through the last couple hours of the flight. More so, the kindness the woman showed me during a particularly stressful time in my life rejuvenated me. Instead of feeling like a pariah, for a moment I felt like we were all in it together. She was able to offer strength in a moment when I felt weak.

I'm happy to say that I was able to return the favor in identical circumstances when I saw a newborn crying on a plane with frazzled parents. I also make it a habit to ask "how can I help?" not only when I see parents struggling with children but anytime I see a situation that could use an extra pair of hands. Often times my offers to help are rebuffed, but that's okay. It helps to empower me, when earlier I would have felt powerless to end the suffering of even minor annoyances. The simple offer "how can I help?" can be the magic deployed when we're irritated with how someone else is handling a harmful situation.

The Protocol for Help

A friend of mine once taught me this bit of common sense. It is so simple that you won't find it written down in most places, but it is incredibly difficult to follow. It goes like this:

Step 1) Ask the person if he or she needs help.

Step 2) If the person consents, help the person but only to the extent that the person wants help and no more.

Step 3) If the person does not consent to help, do not administer any help whatsoever. Why? You can empower someone with help, but you can also *take away* someone's power by helping him or her.

The harm of excessive help was once explained to me by a friend who was confined to a wheelchair. He explained to me the anguish of having people constantly leap to open doors for him when he wanted to feel autonomous; he wanted to work on his physical ability to open doors himself. He told me he wished people would ask before helping. I'm sure all of us have had an overzealous friend or loved one try to help us and accidentally steal personal autonomy in the process. It happens to me and my amazing husband, who is an incredible cook. When I am in the kitchen he fairly vibrates with the desire to help me prepare the meal. I am many wonderful things, but a good cook is not one of them. Yet I'd still much rather have the fun of ruining a meal myself and learning some things about cooking in the process rather than be bored and lose attention while somebody else takes over for me. He's now learned to ask me before rendering assistance.

When you offer your own practical help to others, dear readers, be sure to ask first. And yes, this includes offering advice as well—ask first. It will help show the intended recipient that you are working toward the spirit of empowering and helping them, and it will lower their defenses. And even before you offer advice or help to others, get connected with your spiritual side and see if the divine is leading you toward helping others. Pray or meditate, and be sure to check your own resources first to make sure you have enough to give. Allowing time and space for spiritual guidance can make any opportunity to help others feel like a holy quest. Every morning I pray to be led to those who could be helped best by me. In this way, I feel I am drawn to more people who are suited to receive my guidance or assistance. Or perhaps I keep my eyes peeled more when I believe it's a spiritual duty to do so. Either way, it results in more help and less harm all around.

Small Communities

The other day I spoke with an ex-minister about what we thought would be the key to saving the world and helping the poor. He spoke about the great good that churches have done by consolidating money and disbursing it to those greatest in need. I feel good about how churches have done wonderful things like drives and other community involvement, pooling resources to help a greater number of people. On the other hand, we both noticed how thinly these resources are spread and how it's tough when the reach falls short. I listened with interest about what sorts of things his congregation had done to combat the problem of homelessness within a large city. I realized that within my own smaller worship community is a homeless member and another who is very impoverished. Since they are in such a small community, there's no way those people could ever starve, because they would have to do so in the faces of their very close friends. We gladly hand over groceries and offer space in our homes to these people because we're basically family. I wonder how much better off some of the strangers on the streets would be if they could be drawn in as members of their own small communities.

I believe working within small communities, rather than on a global level, may be one practical way to reduce harm in this world. It's easy to get overwhelmed, even on a small scale. We live in an amazing, growing world with unprecedented communication and travel capabilities granted to nearly everyone. However, some of these new means of communication can also be incredibly alienating. The Internet can make people feel so close and yet so isolated and alone at the same time. On a social networking site I noticed a childhood friend of mine looking rather thin in a photo, and I commented that I was worried about his health. He replied that I was the first person to remark about his struggle (which turned out to be anorexia) and that included acquaintances who see him every day. However, I was so geographically and socially distant from him at the time that I felt completely powerless to help him. Ours is a strange world, that people far away seem close and people close seem far away.

The good news is that we do have the power to reach out to people within our small communities. These communities take many forms: they can be literal communities like neighborhoods or gatherings like prayer circles, meditation groups, pubs, athletic teams, small online forums, or any group of people who bond in their own authentic ways.

What I'm asking you to do now is become a part of one or several small communities. If there are no suitable communities around you, form one of your own. I started my own small meditation group that meets weekly in my home. I wanted it to be something very laid back I could lead even with everything else going on in my life. Over time, it became so much more to the attendees than sitting in mindfulness. We bonded and now help each other out through thick and thin. When one person is having a problem that another or a group of us can solve, we work together to solve it. It's that perfect love and perfect trust within the group that allows each individual to open up about suffering and the rest of us to feel called to relieve it.

The following spiritual exercise can draw together a group of like-minded people. They can become your spiritual kinfolk in your quest to live without harm.

Creating Community Exercise

For this exercise you'll need some colored string, such as embroidery floss. This exercise is best performed during the waxing moon, as it represents the slow gathering of energy and people that comprise the small community's life force. This exercise is also best performed while looking at the moon, if at all possible. You'll be weaving a friendship bracelet while looking at the moon, hoping that your new friends will be looking at that same moon. It's okay too if you're gazing at an overcast sky. I know this because the weather outside Seattle is often overcast, and I've practiced under these conditions quite often.

Seat yourself in meditation and quiet your mind for a few minutes. Set a timer if you wish. When you feel relaxed, you can ground yourself and begin to work with your threads. Think carefully about what sorts of traits you want to see in the people in your community. Select colors of threads that are meaningful to you. For example, pink threads could represent kindness and love. Green threads might represent generosity. Purple threads might represent a spiritual nature. Blue threads might represent calm and healing personalities. Red threads might represent passion and energy. Orange threads might represent happiness and success. Yellow threads might represent an intellectual nature or friendship. It's okay if your color interpretations are different from the ones I've suggested here. What matters is that it makes sense to you and that you can recall the meanings when you look at the threads later.

Tie them together with a knotted loop at one end. Then, begin to weave the threads together. You can do this with any friendship bracelet pattern of knots, or with a simple braid if you don't know how to weave friendship bracelets. As you weave, try to visualize a vibrant community. Imagine yourself laughing and feeling at home with your friends. Try to bring up the feelings you sense when you are with people you truly feel are family. When you have woven enough to make a bracelet or an anklet for yourself, tie it off around the beginning loop on yourself and trim the end strings. Wear the bracelet until it falls off to draw the community to you. Remember that you'll have to do the work as well. Post notices everywhere you can about forming a group of your interest. It can be a meditation group, a prayer group, a community service group, or anything you like. Just do the work and put out your intentions to form what you want in your local community.

Help Those You Know

The most practical advice of all, of course, is to reach out to those closest to you. As mentioned earlier, there are people in my worship group experiencing hardships like homelessness and poverty. But we aren't helping them just to avoid witnessing their suffering; we also know these people well enough to know what sorts of assistance would suit their personalities best. There is no one-size-fits-all end to suffering and harm. You already know that what brings extreme harm to one person might merely annoy or be barely noticed by another. This is why it is best to reach out first to those you know who may need help.

As it happens, the homeless friend I know is an old-school hippie, the type who raised his kids in a school bus turned into a makeshift home. He's now retired and is certainly no pity project. He would never sign up for any kind of aid program that would hem him in, require him to register his name and curtail his freedoms in any way. This is why his most trusted friends can help him best. During the winter he can house-sit for me, and I benefit from his amazing handyman skills. I always come back to a house that is cleaner and in better working order than when I left. My other friend who is suffering from poverty is also not eligible for social services. She's taking care of her elderly mother, who isn't a blood relation. Because she could technically get a job, she isn't eligible for many social services, and they get by on a shared fixed income. We help her out by sharing groceries with her, when we can. Unfortunately she is unable to accept many of the opportunities we offer her due to her obligation as caregiver for her mother.

It would be wonderful if an organized effort of bagged sandwiches and rows of warm beds could help out all of the homeless people on the streets today, but the real people behind the surface of suffering have so many different life stories that may preclude them from accepting anonymous assistance from an organization with rules and limitations.

My point here is that people are individuals with their own life stories. Those who are closest to you may be suffering in ways great and small, and you are in the best position to find sympathy for them. Others in my close community have much smaller problems, like one individual who needed a car during a time when we were able to sell an extra car at reduced cost. Small favors that don't create a great drain on a person are greatly fulfilling.

To close this section, I'd like to offer a prayer I recite every morning to draw people in need closer to me. I offer this prayer so I will notice every opportunity to be of assistance with my simple actions. Such opportunities are like a seeing a bird in a window. If you are able to look and see the bright colors and the wings before it takes flight, you can be forever blessed. You can open the window and allow the bird (happiness) to enter your life. But if your head is turned away, you will never know it was there. The bird will fly away unseen.

The morning prayer goes thusly:

Let those who are in need be drawn to me.
And may I have the strength to know and see.
Give me strength and responsibility
Duty in line with my ability.

Things don't always work out perfectly, of course, but that's why I make a habit of saying this prayer. There are always going to be moments of failure that expose us to a little bit of harm, even if only the emotional type. We have to be daring and follow our true will in life. There may be times when the value of potential help may outweigh the potential for harm. You'll have to reach out and take risks only so much as you can spare. Just as you wouldn't buy a lottery ticket with your last dollar, you shouldn't necessarily help someone with the last ounce of strength you have unless it's a calculated effort. Give what you can, but only what can be spared within your own ability.

Once you speak the prayer, it is your duty to look through your list of friends for people who may be hurting or in trouble. In our modern world, loyalty is a hard thing to find. It's easy to find new friends on the Internet who suit your interests, but it is much harder to reconnect with old friends who may have drifted away from you. On the other hand, you probably have friends already in your sphere of influence that could use a call from you. Perhaps you know somebody who has needs in body, mind, or spirit. Is there someone on your list who could use a bag of groceries or a basket of fresh home-baked goods? Does anyone in your life need a handwritten letter or a simple phone call to be reminded that someone cares? Now is your opportunity to change the world, one person at a time. Truly, one of the universe's greatest gifts is knowing that you don't have to wait one more minute to make the world a better place.

Conclusion

Something has inspired you to consider the spiritual injunction to live with compassion. The directive is so universal and inarguable. It is believed by some to be an inalienable right to every living being and a duty as well to the same universal group. At the same time, completely harming nothing is impossible; with every breath we take and no matter what we do, tiny organisms are obliterated from existence. Why, then, is the idea of being harmless and totally compassionate such a light in the darkness? Why does it attract us like moths to the potential spiritual flame of disappointment and even destruction? Perhaps the answer is not supposed to be simple. Humans possess intellect and the amazing ability to reason, even against one another. Perhaps the very purpose of this drive for us is to use that intellect and debate issues at length. Perhaps the process of understanding and moving ever closer toward the impossibility that is true compassion is greater than its actual achievement. Perhaps a divine source gave us this duty to bring us closer to it and each other.

As you go forward in your attempts, I will not pray that you succeed entirely in your quest; to do so would rob you of the experience of growth. Instead, I pray you do the best you can do to the best of your ability to understand what you need to understand at this point in time. Your idea of compassion right now may be different from your ideas about it in ten or twenty years' time. Indeed, harm itself won't be relevant for us after our lifetimes. On a planetary level, things are very different, perhaps more complex than we can conceive. It is my hope that each of us will be a piece of the puzzle that helps the future become the picture it was meant to be. Good luck to you. Good luck to all of us.

Recommended Reading List

Alvarez, Melissa. *365 Ways to Raise Your Frequency: Simple Tools to Increase Your Spiritual Energy for Balance, Purpose, and Joy.* Woodbury, MN: Llewellyn Worldwide, 2012.

Aurelius, Marcus. *Thoughts of Marcus Aurelius Antonius,* ed. George Long. Kindle edition. Seattle: Amazon Digital Services, 2011.

Batterson, Mark. *The Circle Maker: Praying Circles Around Your Biggest Dreams and Greatest Fears.* Grand Rapids, MI: Zondervan, 2011.

Brown, Brene. *The Gifts of Imperfection: Let Go of Who You Think You're Supposed to Be and Embrace Who You Are.* Center City, MN: Hazelden, 2010.

Chauran, Alexandra. *365 Ways to Strengthen Your Spirituality: Simple Ways to Connect With the Divine.* Woodbury, MN: Llewellyn Publications, 2015.

Duerr, Maia. "The Tree of Contemplative Practices" at The Center for Contemplative Mind in Society. Last Accessed March 27, 2015. http://www.contemplativemind.org /practices/tree.

Dyer, Wayne. *Your Sacred Self: Making the Decision to Be Free.* New York: HarperCollins, 1995.

Mathiesen, Robert, and Theitic. *Rede of the Wiccae.* Newport, RI: The Witches' Almanac, 2005.

Millman, Dan. *No Ordinary Moments: A Peaceful Warrior's Guide to Daily Life.* Tiburon, CA: HJ Kramer, 1992.

Wood, Robin. *When, Why ... If.* Dearborn, MI: Livingtree, 1996.

Bibliography

Backman, Linda. *The Evolving Soul: Spiritual Healing Through Past Life Exploration.* Woodbury, MN: Llewellyn Publications, 2014.

Bayles, Corliss. "Using Mindfulness in a Harm Reduction Approach to Substance Abuse Treatment: A Literature Review." *International Journal of Behavioral Consultation & Therapy* 9.2, 2014: 22–25. Last accessed March 26, 2015. http://psycnet.apa.org/journals/bct/9/2/22 .pdf&productCode=pa.

Bitkoff, Stewart. *A Commuter's Guide to Enlightenment.* Woodbury, MN: Llewellyn Publications, 2008.

Crowther, Patricia. *Lid Off the Cauldron: A Wicca Handbook.* Somerset, UK: Capall Bann Publishing, 1998.

Dale, Cyndi. *The Spiritual Power of Empathy: Develop Your Intuitive Gifts for Compassionate Connection.* Woodbury, MN: Llewellyn Publications, 2014.

Day, Helen. "Engaging Staff to Deliver Compassionate Care and Reduce Harm." *British Journal of Nursing* 23.18, 2014: 974–980. Last accessed March 26, 2015. http://www.ncbi.nlm.nih.gov/pubmed/25302836.

Decker, James T., et al. "Mindfulness, Compassion Fatigue, and Compassion Satisfaction Among Social Work Interns." *Social Work & Christianity* 42.1, 2015: 28–42. Last accessed March 26, 2015. http://www.nacsw.org/RC/49993999.

Greenwood, Carmel. *Letting Go and Loving Life: How to Attract Energy and Abundance … And Relax Enough to Enjoy It.* New York: New American Library, 2002.

Higgs, Robert, and Elizabeth Bernard Higgs. "Compassion—A Critical Factor for Attaining and Maintaining a Free Society." *Independent Review* 19.4, 2015: 627–630. Last accessed March 26, 2015. http://www.independent.org/publications/tir/article.asp?a=1058.

Jazaieri, Hooria, Geshe Thupten Jinpa, Kelly McGonigal, et al. "Enhancing Compassion: A Randomized Controlled Trial of a Compassion Cultivation Training Program." *Journal Of Happiness Studies* 14.4, 2013: 1113–1126. *Psychology and Behavioral Sciences Collection.* Last accessed March 26, 2015. http://ccare.stanford.edu/article /enhancing-compassion-a-randomized-controlled-trial -of-a-compassion-cultivation-training/.

Mathers, S. Liddell MacGregor. *The Key of Solomon the King (Clavicula Salomonis).* York Beach, ME: Weiser Books, 2000.

McConnell, Elizabeth. "Compassion Starts from Within: Beyond the Checklist." *Nursing & Residential Care* 17.2, 2015: 96–99. Last accessed March 26, 2015. http://www.magonlinelibrary.com/doi /abs/10.12968/nrec.2015.17.2.96.

Meyer, Fred. *Don't Give Up Until You Do: From Mindfulness to Realization on the Buddhist Path.* Woodbury, MN: Llewellyn Publications, 2012.

Smeets, Elke, Kristin Neff, et al. "Meeting Suffering With Kindness: Effects of a Brief Self-Compassion Intervention for Female College Students." *Journal of Clinical Psychology* 70.9, 2014: 794–807. *Psychology and Behavioral Sciences Collection.* Last accessed March 26, 2015. http://www.ncbi.nlm.nih.gov /pubmed/24691680.

Wheeler, Evangeline A., and Nathan W. Lenick. "Brief Compassion Meditation and Recall of Positive-Emotion Words." *Journal of Articles in Support of the Null Hypothesis* 11.2, 2015: 11–20. Last accessed March 26, 2015. http://www.jasnh.com/pdf/Vol11-No2-article1.pdf.

Whitehurst, Tess. *The Good Energy Book: Creating Harmony and Balance for Yourself and Your Home.* Woodbury, MN: Llewellyn Publications, 2013.

Wojton, Djuna. *Karmic Choices: How Making the Right Decisions Can Create Enduring Joy.* Woodbury, MN: Llewellyn Publications, 2014.

To Write to the Author

If you wish to contact the author or would like more information about this book, please write to the author in care of Llewellyn Worldwide Ltd. and we will forward your request. Both the author and publisher appreciate hearing from you and learning of your enjoyment of this book and how it has helped you. Llewellyn Worldwide Ltd. cannot guarantee that every letter written to the author can be answered, but all will be forwarded. Please write to:

Alexandra Chauran
℅ Llewellyn Worldwide
2143 Wooddale Drive
Woodbury, MN 55125-2989

Please enclose a self-addressed stamped envelope for reply, or $1.00 to cover costs. If outside the USA, enclose an international postal reply coupon.

Many of Llewellyn's authors have websites with additional information and resources. For more information, please visit our website at http://www.llewellyn.com.

GET MORE AT LLEWELLYN.COM

Visit us online to browse hundreds of our books and decks, plus sign up to receive our e-newsletters and exclusive online offers.

- • Free tarot readings • Spell-a-Day • Moon phases
- • Recipes, spells, and tips • Blogs • Encyclopedia
- • Author interviews, articles, and upcoming events

GET SOCIAL WITH LLEWELLYN

Find us on
Facebook
www.Facebook.com/LlewellynBooks

Follow us on

www.Twitter.com/Llewellynbooks

GET BOOKS AT LLEWELLYN

LLEWELLYN ORDERING INFORMATION

"Through beautifully written vignettes and simple yet powerful reflections, Sara Wiseman helps us step into the flow of grace."

—TARA BRACH, PhD, author of *Radical Acceptance*

Living a Life of Gratitude

✦ ✦ ✦

Your Journey to Grace, Joy & Healing

Sara Wiseman

Living a Life of Gratitude
Your Journey to Grace, Joy & Healing
SARA WISEMAN

When you walk through life with gratitude and simply appreciating everything, every single thing, you reconnect with what's truly important in life. The awe and wonder of life is now ever present.

Through 88 illuminating short stories, *Living a Life of Gratitude* will help you slow down, look around, and see your life for what it is. From our first breaths to our last, Sara Wiseman explores the landmarks of human experience: that we are able to be children and have children, that we can learn and love! Even if we have little, we have so much. Read this book, and revel in the beauty of the world.

978-0-7387-3753-9, 384 pp., 5 x 7   **$16.99**
